Custom Slipcovers
made easy

Elizabeth Dubicki

©2007 Elizabeth Dubicki

Published by

krause publications
An Imprint of F+W Publications

700 East State Street • Iola, WI 54990-0001
715-445-2214 • 888-457-2873
www.krausebooks.com

Our toll-free number to place an order or obtain
a free catalog is (800) 258-0929.

The following registered trademark terms and companies appear in this publication:
Velcro®, Waverly, Calico Corners, Wrights and Prym Consumer USA.

Library of Congress Control Number: 2007924846

ISBN-13: 978-0-89689-710-6

Designed by Heidi Bittner-Zastrow

Edited by Tracy L. Conradt

Printed in China

Dedication

I dedicate this book to my husband Dave,
with love and gratitude for all of his domestic engineering
during many months of slipcover mania.

Acknowledgments

It was again my pleasure to work with a talented team from Krause Publications: acquisitions editor Candy Wiza; book editor Tracy Conradt; graphic designer Heidi Bittner-Zastrow, and studio photographers Kris Kandler and Robert Best. Thank you all for supporting this project through all phases of production. Kudos, as well, to location photographer Kevin May, and big hugs to my photo stylists and all around slipcover soul mates, Mary Baggott and Ellen Naylor.

Finally, I am very grateful to Waverly, Calico Corners, Wrights and Dritz (Prym Consumer USA) for sending me bolts and bolts of wonderful fabrics and boxes of helpful notions. See the Contributors on page 00 for source information. I urge you to seek out the excellent fabrics and sewing aids offered by these companies. Using their products and services will make your slipcover experiences so much better.

Contents

Introduction: A Slipcover Tale...6

Chapter 1:

Decisions, Decisions 8

Take My Chair Challenge.........................9
Choose Your Chair 10
Select Your Fabric 14
Make Style Decisions 17
Gather Notions and Supplies 21
Establish a Project Timeline 22

Chapter 2:

Measuring, Drawing Layouts, and Calculating Yardages 23

Learn Some New Terms 24
Take Basic Measurements 24
Determine Shell and
   Cushion Panel Cutting Dimensions.....28
Determine Skirt Panel
   Cutting Dimensions...........................29
Draw Sample Layouts 32
Consider Yardage Exceptions..................35
Determine Yardages of Other Materials ..38
Pre-Clean and Pre-Cut Your Fabric..........39

Chapter 3:

Making Welting; Making Cushion Covers.. 40

Revive Your Cushions 41
Make New Inner Cushions 42
Make the Welting 43
Construct a Basic Box-Edge
   Cushion Cover 45
Make a Mock-Box Cushion Cover 49
Make a Knife-Edge Cushion Cover 51
Make a Bolster Pillow Cover 53

Chapter 4:

Constructing the Slipcover Shell.................. 55

Remember the General Instructions...... 56
Fit and Assemble the Inner Shell.......... 57
Use Alternate Deck Construction.......... 64
Attach the Outer Shell...................... 65

● Chapter 5:

Adding the Skirt and Creating Closures 67

Learn the Basics and Go Beyond........... 68
Cut and Assemble the Skirt Panels 69
Create Different Hem Edges 71
Attach the Skirt to the Shell 77
Install the Zipper 78
Make Different Closures...................... 79

● Chapter 6:

Fitting Slopes, Curves, Angles and More 82

Make a Sofa Slipcover 83
Address Semi-Detached Back
    and/or Seat Cushions 87
Fit Different Arm Styles....................... 89
Work Around an Exposed Frame 103

● Chapter 7:

Done-in-a-Day Covers.....107

No More Sticky Vinyl 108
Made-for-the-Shade.......................... 110
Grill Cover-up.................................... 113
Chair Back Cover 117
Chair Seat Cover 119
Fitted Table Covers 121
Better Head (and Comfy Feet) 124
Dog House Re-Do 127
Double Dishin' 131
Ironing Day Fun................................. 134

Appendix:

Furniture Dimensions Chart................ 136
Shell and Cushion
    Panel Cutting Chart 138
Skirt Panel Cutting Dimensions.......... 140
54" Fabric Layout Grid 142
60" Fabric Layout Grid 142
Bias Strip Yields................................. 142
Fabric and Notions Checklist 142
Contributors 143
Resources.. 143

Introduction: A Slipcover Tale

Slipcovers have always played an important role in my mother's decorating strategy and, in fact, have influenced her approach to furniture acquisition. "Buy new furniture only when it's top-of-the-line and can be purchased at a deep, deep discount," says my mother. Otherwise, you can make do with what you have through repair, repainting or recovering, many times with a slipcover. Inherent in her strategy, too, is the family motto: *Never give furniture away to strangers…it must be redistributed within the family.*

One example of family redistribution involves a large-scale, high-backed, custom-made sofa originally upholstered in soft white wool. This one-of-a-kind piece would have been beyond my parents' budget had not the original buyer reneged on the purchase. They picked up this deeply discounted sofa several years before I was born, and it remained a staple in their furniture repertoire for the next 30 years.

White wool isn't practical in a family of growing children, so my mother had the sofa slip-covered in extravagant pink-and-green floral chintz. The colors of this bold print can be imagined even in the old black-and-white family photo below.

You can make do with the furniture you have, says my mother, by recovering it with a slipcover.

When I was in grade school, my mother changed her color palette to neutral beige, and the sofa was transformed with a simple off-white linen slipcover. A few years later, as the nation segued into harvest gold and avocado green, she redid the sofa in dusty gold cotton damask. This slipcover lasted more than 15 years, largely because she took excellent care of the fabric with cold water laundering and air drying on the basement clothesline. In those days, slipcovers were fitted ultra-tight, so she would always redress the sofa when the fabric was slightly damp and a bit stretchy.

During my high school years, Mom recovered the sofa in black-and-white houndstooth upholstery and moved it to the family room where it became the teenage slouch couch and gathering spot for TV shows and popcorn. Then, as we children grew up and began moving out on our own, redistribution began.

One January day in the mid-1970s, my father waved a $10 bill at a young man who happened to be standing near the freight elevator in my apartment building. He soon found himself

Forget the cute baby in front of the sofa (yes, that's me). Take a gander at that fabulous slipcover fabric and imagine its impact on a 9-foot sofa!

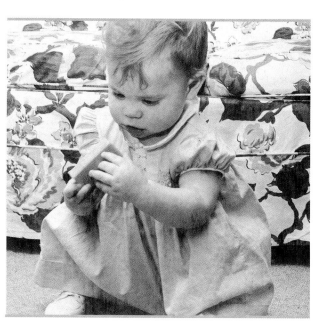

Mrs. Huston made these chair and sofa slipcovers for my parents in the late '70s, and they still look great today. The English floral print came from Calico Corners' retail store in St. Louis.

hoisting one end of this mammoth sofa as he and Dad negotiated its girth in and out of the elevator, around corners, down hallways and through the narrow front door of my first Chicago apartment. My father was glad to see it go, but I was ecstatic. The sofa was mine, all mine!

I bought 16 yards of oatmeal-colored kettle cloth and a few more yards of navy velveteen for the welting, and got to work on a new slipcover. Although I had never made a slipcover, I had witnessed many transformations in my parent's home, including the excellent work of Mrs. Huston, the seamstress who periodically moved in with her sewing machine and stayed for days (even weeks) constructing new slipcovers when my mother felt like a redo.

"How hard can this be?" I thought at the time, with the smug confidence of a sewer who began making her clothes in the sixth grade. I quickly realized the truth of this adage: *Confidence is what you have before you understand the problem.* I charged in with big scissors and made some big mistakes, which sent me back to the fabric store for extra yardage. In the end, my oatmeal slipcover with navy welting looked good enough for a single gal's first apartment, and I was able to conceal the really noticeable goofs with pillows and afghans.

If you're a sewer who has the skills, but lacks the confidence to tackle a full-blown slipcover project, you are my reader!

After this first debacle, I read up on slipcovermaking, took a class on the subject, and went on to make many slipcovers during the ensuing years, including two projects featured in national sewing publications. I've learned through practice, trial and error what works and what doesn't, and have honed some techniques to streamline the construction process. I think Mrs. Huston would approve of my slipcovers today.

Herein lies the nexus of this book. If you're a sewer who has the skills, but lacks the confidence to tackle a full-blown slipcover project, *you* are my reader! I'll walk you through the measuring, fitting and construction nuances of this craft. In the end, you will have the *confidence* to create your own slipcover masterpieces! Along the way, if you find yourself buying in to my family's tradition of furniture redistribution (as evidenced by many of the projects in this book), welcome to the clan!

And what happened to the famous sofa? When I moved to my second Chicago apartment, the sofa was relocated to my sister's home in a northern suburb. (Ellen and sofa have moved twice since then.) Today, this still functional lounge wears a tweed slipcover in soft sage and takes up one whole wall of Ellen's cozy TV den.

Redistribution continues in my family as the grandchildren are growing up and moving out. It remains to be seen where this sofa will end up—and what its next slipcover will be!

Chapter 1
Decisions, Decisions

This chair and its slipcover serve as a reference for discussion in this chapter and as the tutorial project for construction techniques given in Chapters 2 through 5.

Take My Chair Challenge

Just about any piece of upholstered furniture can take a slipcover. This is a bold statement, and I stand by it for the simple reason that wherever fabric is used on the underlying furniture, a fabric slipcover can go on top.

However, just because a piece of furniture can be slipcovered, it doesn't necessarily mean the piece is a wise choice for sewers who are new to the craft. For your first slipcover project, *I suggest you choose an upholstered chair that has at least one detached cushion (seat, back, or both).*

In the chapters that follow, I'll introduce you to universal techniques for making a slipcover that covers the entire chair, including the loose cushion(s). After practicing these techniques on your first project, you will be ready to take on larger, more involved projects, such as loveseats and sofas.

The following guidelines will help you select your chair. Refer to them again when you're ready to start other slipcover projects.

Choose Your Chair

In choosing the chair (or any piece of furniture for a slipcover project), ask yourself the following questions; your answers will guide your selection.

- **Is it in good enough condition to be covered?** A seat that sags or underlying filler material that feels crunchy or is misshaped are signs that the potential chair needs its springs retied and fillers replaced. A slipcover won't mask these problems. The same is true of wiggly arms or a rocky frame. Unless you're prepared to make major structural repairs yourself, don't spend the time, money and effort on a chair that isn't worthy of a slipcover.

The exception, of course, is a treasured heirloom or a really cool vintage piece that falls into the category of "priceless." Only you know the chair's value, so repair the chair's infrastructure, if you must, before you slipcover it.

- **Does it have an exposed frame?** Yes, you can put fabric over wood, metal or plastic furniture frames, but *without* a decent amount of upholstery fabric to cling to in other areas, a slipcover will slide around on the frame surfaces. All of that sliding around means you'll have to readjust the cover each time someone sits in the chair … and the fabric will probably get creased or wrinkled in the process. Too much work! Too messy! You are better off creating a partial slipcover for chairs with exposed frames (chair seat or chair back). See the Done-in-a-Day projects in Chapter 7 for examples.

Don't worry about stains and threadbare fabric on the underlying upholstery, which are obvious flaws of the chair pictured above. A chair that stands well on four legs and is in good shape otherwise qualifies for a slipcover.

Thumbs up for a full slipcover: *Even though this chair has an exposed wood frame, there is still enough underlying upholstery to carry off a full slipcover. The fabric, terry cloth chenille, has the added tactile advantage of a rough wrong side, which helps the cover stay in place, even over the wood surfaces.*

Thumbs down for a full slipcover: *Too much wood and not enough upholstery render this chair as a seat-only slipcover candidate. The back and arms are just too bony! See Chair Seat Cover on page 119 for instructions to make this seat-only project.*

• **Does it have sloped arms, wings or other curved edges?** In general, the more curves you have to cover, the more fitting you'll have to do. For your first project, look for square corners and right angles. In other words, make a slipcover for a club or tuxedo-style chair and save your grandmother's asymmetrical sloped back fainting couch as a future project.

Check out the angles: This square-shaped club chair (above) and the tuxedo-styled sofa (left) are probably the easiest furniture styles to cover ... and this is why I selected the club chair for your tutorial project.

Consider the curves: Chairs like these can be slipcovered—in fact, they're wearing them! (The blue linen cover was made by me; the black floral cover was made by my mentor, Mrs. Huston.) You, too, can make covers like these after you master some basic techniques. When you're ready to segue from square to curvaceous, consult Chapter 6 for fitting techniques to address slopes, curves and funky angles.

- **Is it musty or moldy?** Do a sniff test. No amount of spray-on fabric freshener will eliminate an icky smell, so reject an odoriferous chair.

- **Does it have moving parts?** An upholstered chair that swivels or rocks and has its moving parts concealed by a skirt is acceptable. Recliners, on the other hand, require careful slipcover engineering and are beyond the scope of this book.

- **Is it covered in vinyl or leather?** Some manufacturers offer slipcovers for their leather furniture, but I question how well these covers stay in place. Unless you make your cover extra tight, you may find that it needs readjusting after each "sit." Experiment by wrapping medium-weight woven fabric around the seat and inside back, and then take several good "sits" to see if the leather-fabric combination is acceptable.

- **Are the detached cushions in good shape?** You don't have to reject a chair with good bones just because the cushions are too pooped to plump. New foam and batting innards covered in muslin is an easy and cost-effective way to make your chair's cushions look brand new. See Make New Inner Cushions on page 42 in Chapter 3 to learn how to build a new cushion from the foam outward.

The seat cushion shown was down-filled (so soft!), which spoke well of the quality of this chair. Instead of replacing this cushion, I patched the frayed sections of its original cover with scrap fabric.

Select Your Fabric

Commercially made slipcovers, both the toss-and-tuck kind as well as the custom covers offered by some furniture manufacturers, are typically made from durable, cleanable fabrics. The most commonly used fabrics, in my study of commercial offerings, are medium-weight, solid-colored cotton canvas and brushed twills. I've also noticed a few stripes, some "tweed" types in cotton/poly blends, and a smattering of microfiber suede. Only occasionally, have I run across a print, which is usually of the faded floral tea-stained shabby-chic genre.

While these fabrics do make excellent slipcovers, they are offered in a limited range of neutral or "safe" colors. Here's your chance to break out of this limited palette of hues and ho-hum patterns to create fabrications that reflect your personal decorating style.

Go/sew for it!

As you shop for slipcover fabric, ask yourself this basic question: *How will the slipcovered chair (sofa, etc.) be used?* High traffic chairs need sturdy fabric that stays in place, lasts a long time and is easily cleaned, preferably in your washing machine. Low traffic chairs—those infrequently used accent pieces—can afford more finicky fabrics. Please refer to the fabric criteria and suggestions on the following pages as you make your selection.

Geometric designs, solids and prints … there are so many fabrics from which to choose! Just be sure to select a stable woven fabric that will hold up to use over time and won't stretch out of shape when fitted to your furniture—and sat upon!

Fabric Do's

- Select fabric that is 54" or 60" wide.
- Choose a stable (closely woven) medium-weight fabric with a good hand.
- Look for primarily natural fiber content, like cotton, linen, silk and wool. Blends are fine, too. Some 100-percent synthetic materials may neither take a crease nor forget an inadvertently pressed one, which can be a problem if you desire crisp pleats in your slipcover skirt. I suggest you use synthetic fabric only for very tailored covers, those *without* plentiful pleats, gathers, or ruffles.
- Consider these fabric types:
    - Linen
    - Cotton canvas or cotton duck
    - Cotton twill
    - Denim
    - Corduroy
    - Faux suede
    - Non-knit-backed velour
    - Suit-weight wool and wool blends
    - Screened or woven prints and stripes
    - Damask
    - Jacquard
    - Chenille upholstery types
    - Silk taffeta and raw silk (may need to be lined and/or interlined)
    - Terry cloth

Fabric Don'ts

- Set aside lightweight and tissue-weight versions of the fabrics listed … they're too frail and airy for substantial slipcovers.
- Reject stretchy, slinky and clingy fabrics. In other words, do not dress your furniture in lingerie!
- Say "no" to loosely woven fabrics in both natural and synthetic fibers. They will stretch out of shape when you pin-fit and stitch the slipcover panels, and/or they won't hold their shape when you sit on them!
- Call it quits on quilt-weight cottons (however tempting their colors and prints may be). They lack the necessary heft for an oft-used slipcover, and they're just not wide enough to accommodate aesthetic cuts.
- Take a pass on polar fleece. It will stretch, pill and poop out as a cover for furniture. Plus, fleece is thermal, and who wants to sit on a "hot seat"?

Can't decide on one fabric? Bring home swatches of several in your chosen colorway … one will emerge as the "it" print and another may become the accent fabric you use for welting.

Fabric Maybe's

- Fabrics with large repeating prints, naps and/or distinct horizontal or vertical weaves can be used, but will require extra yardage; see Consider Yardage Exceptions on page 35. I give them a "maybe" rating only because they pose yardage calculation and matching challenges for beginning slipcover sewers. But, by all means, use an extravagant print if you love it! I'll help you make the most of your fabric's majestic motifs.

- Opaque fabrics like voile and organza that hint at the underlying chair do appear as slipcovers in home décor magazines from time to time. They look chic, but aren't really practical for everyday living. Should you decide that such a fabric is a must-have, choose a crisp cotton or linen (not a synthetic version) and use it on a "glam" chair (that is, one that's just for show).

- Upholstery-weight fabrics can make beautiful slipcovers, but sewing them may be too hard on your machine. Before you commit to such a fabric, buy ⅛ yard and layer it as follows:
  - Use four layers if you are considering self welting or use six layers if you want self welting and pleats.
  - Take a test drive over the layers of your fabric, and check for even tension and stitch length on the needle and bobbin sides of your stitching lines. Problems in these areas may indicate that your machine does not have enough "oomph" to handle multiple layers of your intended fabric.

Large geometric designs and super-sized prints make divine slipcovers ... but they require extra yardage and careful attention to motif placement and matching. See Consider Yardage Exceptions, beginning on page 35 in Chapter 2, for guidance in these areas.

Take a test drive over your layered fabric to determine if your machine can handle the bulk.

Make Style Decisions

It's all about style these days, and you want your slipcovered chair to fit in—or stand out, depending on your decorating preferences. Study home décor magazines for inspiration. You may decide to use your chair as an accent piece by selecting a fabric in a bold, contrasting color that really catches the eye. Or, you may want your chair to blend in with your existing décor. In this case, pick a fabric that matches or closely resembles other pieces in the same space.

Your chair has its own structural style, but you can punch up some elements, minimize others, and redesign the skirt to substantially alter its appearance. Here are some ways to do this:

- **Use welting made from a contrasting fabric.** Welting made from another fabric draws the eye to the shape of the chair's arms, cushions and overall silhouette. Because the welting fabric is cut on the bias, a vertical stripe becomes a candy cane stripe … neat!

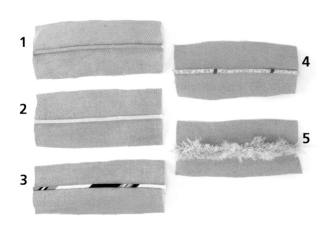

Edgy! These welting samples illustrate very different looks achieved with the following fabrics/trims: matching fabric (no. 1); contrasting solid color fabric (no. 2); coordinating printed fabrics (nos. 3 and 4); and tactile sewn-in fringe (no. 5).

- **Use purchased or custom-made trims instead of welting.** Try outlining your cushions, front arm panels or skirt upper edge with fringe, twisted cord or other trim that's sewn into prominent seams … fun!

The damask slipcover fabric was a bit heavy for welting, so I used solid taupe linen instead. This edge accent draws the eye to the sofa's square silhouette and contrasts nicely with the damask's muted floral design.

I used leftover red tweed fabric from the tutorial chair's slipcover to create the flange welting on this floral loveseat. I like the combination of textured tweed and bountiful bouquets, don't you? See Flange Edges in Chapter 6, page 76, for instructions to make this edge treatment.

• **Change the skirt length and style.** Older upholstered chairs often have short skirts or no skirts at all…just exposed wood legs. Other skirst may have mini-, maxi- or mid-length. They may have pleats or no pleats, gathers or no gathers, or band accents or plain. You're the skirt designer now! See Chapter 2 for yardage calculations and Chapter 4 for instructions to make each of the skirt styles pictured below.

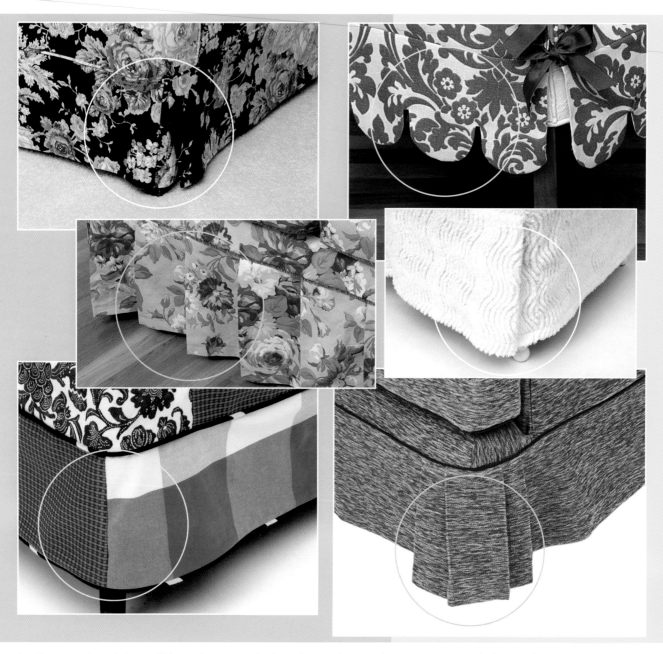

In Chapters 2 and 4, you'll learn how to calculate the yardage and construct several skirts styles, including the ones shown above (clockwise, starting at the upper left): flat skirt with inverted corner pleats; scallop-edged skirt; flat skirt with front corner knife-edge pleats; flat skirt with corner box pleats flanked with knife-edge pleats; flat panel skirt with welted edge; and knife-edge pleated skirt.

- **Change the cushion style—add a cushion—or rehab the old ones with new filler materials.** Making new covers for the loose seat and back cushions is part of the slipcover process. You can recover the existing cushions or do a little redesign by substituting a mock-box, bolster or knife-edge style for the traditional box-edge cushion. Another way to change the look and comfort of older furniture is to pump up the cushion volume with new filler materials. A little cushion rehab can take years off the look of a dated piece of furniture! See Chapter 3 for instructions.

One Room—Two Looks

The same room—two different looks—all achieved through the miracle of slipcovers. How divine!

If you're like me, you acquire furniture over time. This sofa and pair of easy chairs are made by the same manufacturer but were purchased many years apart. Off-white upholstery helps to coordinate their different styles, and the silk accent pillows and Oriental rug in muted gold and greens add subtle color.

Presto! Matching blue linen slipcovers, a needlepoint area rug and some different accessories change the room's attitude. The new slipcovers feature the same skirt treatment and arm front details, which add to the overall unified effect of the space.

Gather Notions and Supplies

Sewing a slipcover does not require a machine upgrade. All you need is a sturdy machine with zigzag stitch capability, an adjustable needle and a zipper foot. Remember to test-stitch multiple layers of your chosen fabric to make sure your machine is up to task.

In addition to your machine, gather or purchase these materials:

Fabric and Notions

- Slipcover and welting fabric(s) in determined yardage
- Cotton cording in determined size and yardage (see Cording Yardage on page 38)
- Metal zipper chain in determined yardage with zipper pulls and stops (see Zipper Chain Yardage on page 38)
- ⅞"-wide fusible-web seam tape (for zipper insertion)
- All-purpose sewing thread
- Size 14, 16 or 18 machine needles (depending on fabric weight)
- Long straight pins with ball heads, T-pin, and corkscrew pins (optional)

Tools

- Scissors: long-blade shears; extra-sharp short-blade scissors; thread clippers; seam ripper; pinking shears (optional)
- 1½"-wide clear plastic yardstick
- Regular and 120"-long tape measures; sewing gauge
- Water-soluble fabric marker (buy two!); tailor's chalk
- Carpenter square
- Large cutting mat
- Cutting table, available for about $100 at fabric stores (optional, but a real plus when making décor projects)

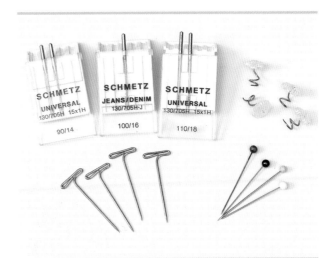

Pins and needles: *Pins bend, needles break. Have lots of them on hand as you begin your project. T-pins are especially important for securing fabric panels to the chair while you fit them. The cork screw pins provide a discreet way to keep a finished cover from shifting.*

Measure and mark: *An extra-long tape measure and the 6" sewing gauge are essential for measuring the long—and the short—of your project. You'll be marking many seams by hand as you fit your cover, so buy extra fabric markers and tailor's chalk.*

Establish a Project Timeline

I remember the days when I could stay up all night to sew a dress for myself (or my daughter) to wear to the party/dance the next day. I used to have the stamina for such sewing marathons, but I've learned from experience that I do not do my best work when I've set an unrealistic time frame for a project, especially a slipcover.

A full slipcover for a chair is *not* a done-in-a-day project; however, it won't take you weeks to complete either. You could make your slipcover over a weekend if you have big blocks of uninterrupted time—and lots of caffeine. But, give yourself a break and break up the construction over several days and several sewing sessions. To help you manage your project efficiently from beginning to end, I've created the following list of tasks to streamline the construction process. Tackle one task (or at the most two tasks) per sewing session, and—hurrah!—you *will* finish your first slipcover.

1 Choose your chair; make style decisions; go shopping for fabric and bring swatches home—fun, fun, fun! (Review Chapter 1.)

2 Measure your chair; draw a sample layout; determine yardage; purchase fabric and notions; gather tools. (See Chapter 2.)

3 Make all required welting for your project; cut out slipcover panels; make covers for loose cushions (Chapter 3).

4 Fit and assemble the inner shell (Chapters 4 and 6).

5 Fit and assemble the outer shell (Chapters 4 and 6).

6 Make and attach the skirt; install the zipper closure (Chapters 5 and 6).

Every craft needs an instructional reference point, and mine is this classic club chair that once was my father's favorite seat for reading the newspaper. So favorite, in fact, that he wore out two upholsteries and one slipcover before I inherited this chair. In Chapters 2, 3, 4 and 5, I've used this chair to illustrate many techniques. However, one chair project cannot address every construction issue. I've also included techniques and instructions for cutting, fitting and assembling covers for other furniture styles, plus some fun details you can add to any slipcover.

Chapter 2

Measuring, Drawing Layouts, and Calculating Yardages

Graph it up, please! Calculating yardage is easy when you take some simple measurements and draw a sample layout.

Measurements

Everyone who sews understands the importance of taking measurements. Drawing a layout, however, may seem remedial, especially for garment makers who rarely consult pattern layouts before cutting. Remember, though, that with a few minor tweaks, the layout not only shows you how much fabric to buy, it provides the cutting dimensions of your slipcover panels. The layout also helps you plan the placements of repeating motifs in print fabrics—and ensures enough yardage to center large floral bouquets (super-sized stripes, prominent geometrics, etc.) within your chair's focal point panels.

Learn Some New Terms

A chair (or any piece of furniture for that matter) and the human body have much in common: arms, legs, backs and seats. The comparison continues between slipcovers and garments, which share skirts, pleats, hems, darts, tucks, gathers as well as zipper, button, or snap closures. These anthropomorphic connections and shared sewing terminology make slipcovering "feel" like garment making (which it is in many respects). I've attempted to use garment sewing terms as well as common terms for furniture parts wherever possible and appropriate to make you feel at home with the process.

However, in some cases I've used poetic license to create a new term to identify a structural seam, a furniture part or a slipcover section. For example, in my vernacular, the juncture of the arm and the inside back of an upholstered chair (or sofa) is the *arm joint*. The upper back corners of an upholstered chair (sans back cushion, if any) are the *shoulders*. The area around the perimeter of the chair seat (sans seat cushion) where you can stick your fingers into is the *tuck-in crevice*. And the fabric cover that fits over a piece of furniture (with cushions removed) is the *slipcover shell*. You'll soon be on a first-name basis with these and other terms as you undertake the initial step of slipcover making, which is: *measuring your chair*.

Take Basic Measurements

Refer to the Chair Anatomy photos and descriptions on the following two pages to identify and measure similar sections of your chair. *Remember:* The blue tape measure indicates **width** and the green tape measure indicates **length**. Take measurements of each section at *its widest and longest points.*

Also, measure the width and length of the top and bottom panels of your chair's detached seat and/or back cushions. Again, take measurements at the widest, longest, and deepest points of the cushions. For example, the width of the top and bottom panel of T-shape cushion should be taken at the outermost edges of the T-extensions. Measure each cushion's perimeter and depth (that is, the cushion's box band, if it has one), as well.

Record all of these measurements in inches in the Furniture Dimensions Chart on page 27. This chart is repeated on page 136 in the Appendix. Feel free to photocopy this chart for use with all of your slipcover projects.

Chair Anatomy Measurements

❶ Inside Back

Measure width and length of the inside back. Note: In this photo and the following photos, the blue tape measure indicates width and the green tape measure indicates length.

❷ Deck

The deck width measurement spans the outer edges of the T-extensions (left and right) and continues over them to the point where the skirt will be attached. The deck length (depth) measurement likewise extends over the deck front edge and down to where the skirt will be attached.

❸ Inside Arm

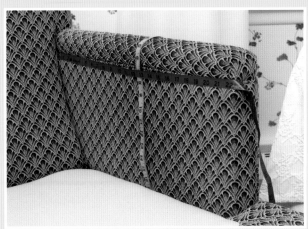

The inside arm panel, after pin-fitting and trimming, will cover the area shown in the primary photo above. However, this panel also covers the entire upper edge of the arm, which adds to this panel's total width and length.

Inside Arm Extra Width

To determine the inside arm panel total width, measure from the arm back edge (where it intersects with the outside back) to the arm front edge, as shown with the blue tape measure in the photo above.

Inside Arm Extra Length

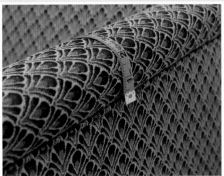

To determine the inside arm panel total length, begin your measurement at the outer welted upholstery seam as shown with the green tape measure in the photo above, and drape your tape measure over the arm upper edge and down to the chair deck.

④ Arm Front

This square arm is easy to measure. For asymmetrical arm shapes, remember to measure the arm front area at its widest and longest points.

⑤ Outside Arm

Skirt Attachment Point

This panel's upper edge and width coincide with the arm's welted edge; its length ends where the skirt will be attached. Follow the upholstery seams of your furniture piece to measure the outside arm area.

⑥ Outside Back

Skirt Attachment Point

Measure the outside back width (at its widest point) and the length (at its longest point) where the skirt will be attached.

⑦ Chair Perimeter

Use an extra-long tape measure to measure the chair's perimeter at the determined point where the skirt will be attached.

⑧ Finished Skirt Length

Skirt Attachment Point

This measurement indicates the finished skirt length. I like my full-length slipcover skirts to skim the floor; however, you may want some clearance between skirt and floor. If so, subtract ½" from the to-the-floor measurement.

⑨ Tuck-In Crevice Depth

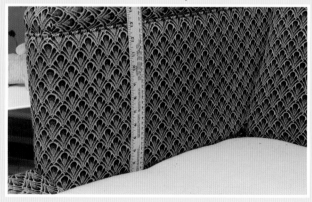

Use a rigid ruler or yardstick to measure the depth of the tuck-in crevice around the side and back edges of the deck. If the depth varies, decide on a uniform depth between 2" and 4".

Furniture Dimensions Chart
(width x length in inches)

Shell Measurements

1 Inside Back   _____" x _____"

2 Deck (including front/side overhang)   _____" x _____"

3 Inside Arm   _____" x _____"

4 Arm Front   _____" x _____"

5 Outside Arm   _____" x _____"

6 Outside Back   _____" x _____"

7 Chair Perimeter (where skirt will be attached)   _____"

8 Finished Skirt Length   _____"

9 Tuck-in Crevice Depth*   _____"

Box-Edge Cushion Measurements**

10 Seat Cushion Top and Bottom Panels   _____" x _____"

11 Seat Cushion Box Band (cushion perimeter x depth)   _____" x _____"

12 Back Cushion Top and Bottom Panels   _____" x _____"

13 Back Cushion Box Band (cushion perimeter x depth)   _____" x _____"

*   If the tuck-in crevice depth varies around the deck, decide on a uniform depth from 2" to 4".

** If making non-box-edge cushion covers, refer to the instructions beginning on page 49 in Chapter 3 for measuring, cutting, and constructing alternative cushion covers.

Determine Shell and Cushion Panel Cutting Dimensions

Use the dimensions noted in the Furniture Dimensions Chart to calculate the panel cutting dimensions and record them in the Panel Cutting Chart below. Even if a chair section is not exactly square or rectangular in shape, for yardage, cutting and fitting purposes, it's important to err on the generous side. This is why I've added ½" seam allowances *and* an extra inch to the width/length of some panels—you will trim excess fabric during construction. The Panel Cutting Chart is repeated on page 00 in the Appendix. You can photocopy it to use with other slipcover projects.

Shell and Cushion Panel Cutting Chart
(width x length in inches)

Shell Panels

1 Inside Back (cut 1)   _____" + 2" x _____" + 2" + No. 9

2 Deck (including front/side overhang) (cut 1)   _____" + 3"+ (*No. 9 x 2*) x _____" + 3"+ (*No. 9*)

3 Inside Arm (cut 2)   _____" + 2" x _____" + 2" + No. 9

4 Arm front (cut 2)*   _____" + 2" x _____" + 2" + No. 9

5 Outside Arm (cut 2)   _____" + 2" x _____" + 2"

6 Outside Back (cut 1)**   _____" + 2" x _____" + 2"

Box-Edge Cushion Panels***

10 Seat Cushion Top and Bottom Panel (cut 2)   _____" + 1" x _____" + 1"

11 Seat Cushion Box Band (piecing as necessary)****   _____" + 4" x _____" + 2"

12 Back Cushion Top and Bottom Panel (cut 2)   _____" + 1" x _____" + 1"

13 Back Cushion Box Band (piecing as necessary)****   _____" + 4" x _____" + 2"

* These cutting dimensions include the tuck-in allowance which is required to accommodate the tutorial chair's T-shaped deck and seat cushion. For other chair/furniture styles, you will trim off some of the length of this panel during construction.

** If making a center back closure (in lieu of the standard back edge zipper closure), see Make Different Closures on page 79 in Chapter 5 before cutting this panel.

*** To determine the panel cutting dimensions of non-box-edge cushions, see the instructions beginning on page 52 in Chapter 3.

**** These are the overall dimensions of the box band panel for purposes of yardage calculation. For specific cutting dimensions, see Construct a Box-Edge Cushion Cover on page 45 in Chapter 3.

Determine Skirt Panel Cutting Dimensions

Skirt construction is covered in detail in Chapter 4, but at this juncture your concern is to have enough fabric to make your desired skirt style. The following formulas will help you calculate both the dimensions and the number of cut panels you will need to make your chosen skirt. (*Note:* These formulas are repeated on page 140–141 in the Appendix.)

Skirt Panel Cut Length
(the same for all skirt styles)

You have already determined your skirt's finished length and noted this figure as the No. 8 measurement in the Furniture Dimensions Chart on page 136. Use this figure in the following formula to determine the cut length (depth) of all of your slipcover's skirt panels; this measurement will be the same regardless of your skirt style.

> *panel cut length (depth) = No. 8 measurement (skirt finished length) + 4½"*

For example, if you have determined that your skirt will have a finished length of 9", the cut length of the skirt panels will be 13½" (9" + 4½").

For traditional flat or pleated skirts, the extra 4½" will be used to create a 2"-deep doubled hem, and the remaining ½" will be used as the seam allowance to join the skirt upper edge to the slipcover shell's lower edge.

For skirts with welted and/or flanged, banded or scalloped hems, 3½" will be used for a hem facing panel or the hem band. The remaining 1" will be used for seam allowances to join the facing and band to the skirt lower edge and to join the skirt upper edge to the slipcover shell's lower edge.

Skirt Total Width

Start with the chair's perimeter measurement at the point where the slipcover skirt will be attached—this is the No. 7 measurement you have noted in the Furniture Dimensions Chart on page 136. To this measurement you will add pleat or gathering allowances plus seam allowances. Use inches in all calculations. *Note:* The following formulas assume a standard zipper closure.

- **For a flat skirt:** Add 8" to the No. 7 measurement. These extra inches are more than enough to join skirt panels at their short edges and stitch the remaining edges in a seam to accommodate a zipper closure.
- **For a gathered skirt:** Multiply the No. 7 measurement by 2 to 2½ , depending on the desired fullness of the skirt. Add 8" to the resulting figure for joining seams and a zipper closure seam.
- **For a skirt with four box or knife-edge pleated corners** (like the tutorial chair's slipcover skirt shown on the next pages), add 64" (16" per pleat) to the No. 7 measurement plus 8" for joining seams and a zipper closure.

- **For a skirt with four inverted corner pleats,** add 48" (12" per pleat) to the No. 7 measurement, plus 8" for joining seams and a zipper closure.

- **For a fully pleated skirt,** first decide on the pleat style (inverted, box or knife-edge) and then determine the desired pleat depth.
  - Experiment by folding scrap fabric into pleats until you're satisfied with the pleat dimensions, then measure the desired pleat depth. (*Example:* A 6"-wide box pleat requires a 12" pleat allowance; a 3"-deep inverted pleat also requires a 12" pleat allowance; a 3"-deep knife pleat requires a 6" pleat allowance.)
  - Decide how many pleats to make (at least 8 pleats, increased by increments of 4 (that is, 8, 12, 16, 20, and so on)
  - Multiply the desired number of pleats by the determined allowance for a single pleat, and then add 8" extra for joining seams and the zipper closure. Add the resulting figure to the No. 7 measurement.

Required Number of Skirt Panels

Record the skirt cut length and width as calculated on page 30. To determine how many skirt panels you will need, use this formula:

total skirt length ÷ fabric width =
number of skirt panels*

*This formula assumes you will cut your skirt panels across the width of your fabric.

For example, assume your slipcover project has a No. 7 measurement of 102" and a No. 8 measurement of 9". Assume, too, that you've decided on a flat skirt style with four box- or knife-edge corner pleats (like the tutorial chair's skirt). Here's how you would calculate the cut length, width and number of skirt panels required to make this skirt:

cut length = No. 8 measurement
(9") + 4½" = 13½"

total width = No. 7 measurement
(102") + pleat allowance (64") +
seam allowances (8") = 174"

required number of skirt panels cut across
fabric width = total width (174") ÷ fabric
width (54") = approximately 3¼ panels

You will use these skirt panel measurements when you draw the sample layout, a process discussed on the following page.

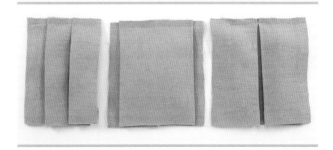

These small sewn samples illustrate the following skirt styles (left to right): knife-edge; box; and inverted.

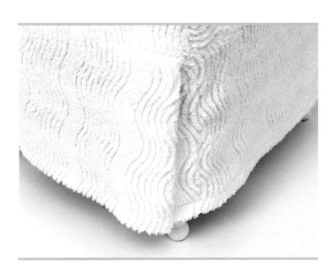

This skirt illustrates a corner knife edge pleat.

Draw Sample Layouts

Straight Grain vs. Railroaded Layout

Garment sewers are accustomed to *straight grain* layouts with the fabric folded in half widthwise, right sides together and selvages aligned. Garment patterns are usually positioned with their grain lines running parallel to the selvages.

It may seem like heresy for sewers ingrained with straight grains, but *railroading* (cutting panels on the cross grain) can help you conserve yardage. It also helps avoid piecing skirt panels, and other shell panels on larger slipcover projects, such as the inside back, outside back, and deck panels of a sofa.

If you're having trouble visualizing these orientations, see the photos below. In the left photo, Ellen has draped the cut end of some yardage over one shoulder, toga-style, with selvages running from her shoulder to the floor. She's wearing this fabric on the *straight grain*. In the right photo, she's wound the same fabric around herself so that the selvages are parallel to the floor. Now she's *railroaded*. Imagine your chair in place of this lovely model. See the difference between these orientations? Good.

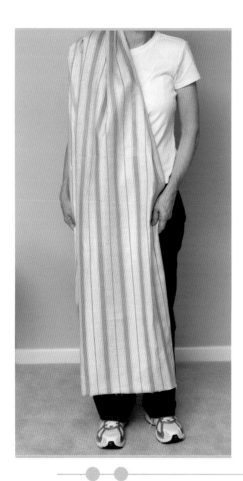 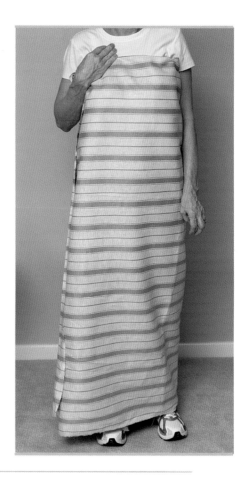

A stripe illustrates the difference between straight grain (left photo) and railroaded (right photo) orientations of fabric.

Sample Layouts

Using the tutorial chair and its slipcover style as an example, I've measured its sections, determined the cut panel dimensions, and have prepared both straight grain and railroaded layouts for a 54"-wide solid fabric. The straight grain layout shows that I will need 8½ yards of 54"-wide fabirc. Per the railroaded layout shown on page 34, I will only need 7 yards of this fabric. Here's the rub: My chosen fabric has a distinct weave that runs across the fabric width, selvage to selvage. So, I must use a straight grain layout to accommodate this weave and this requires extra yardage.

Straight Grain Layout = approx. 8½ yd.

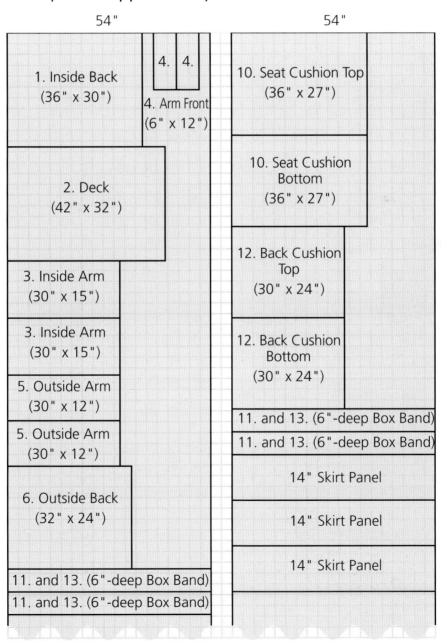

Railroaded Layout = approx. 7 yd.

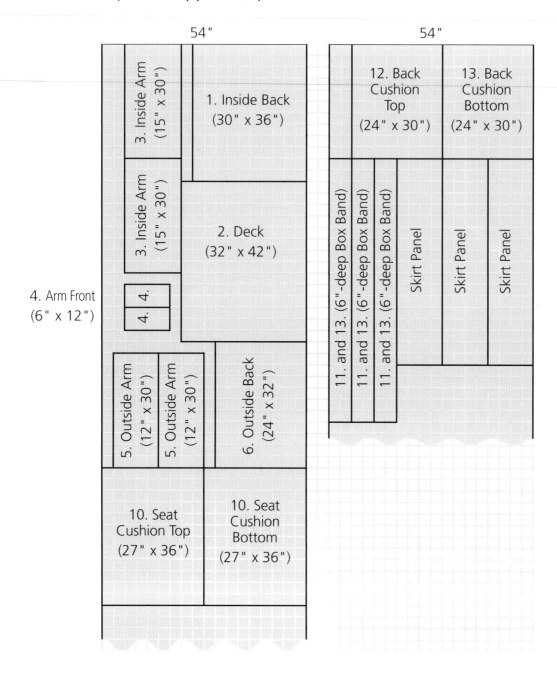

54"

54"

3. Inside Arm
(15" x 30")

3. Inside Arm
(15" x 30")

1. Inside Back
(30" x 36")

2. Deck
(32" x 42")

4. Arm Front
(6" x 12")

4.

4.

5. Outside Arm
(12" x 30")

5. Outside Arm
(12" x 30")

6. Outside Back
(24" x 32")

10. Seat
Cushion Top
(27" x 36")

10. Seat
Cushion
Bottom
(27" x 36")

12. Back
Cushion
Top
(24" x 30")

13. Back
Cushion
Bottom
(24" x 30")

11. and 13. (6"-deep Box Band)

11. and 13. (6"-deep Box Band)

11. and 13. (6"-deep Box Band)

Skirt Panel

Skirt Panel

Skirt Panel

To draw your layout and determine the required yardage, use the Layout Graph in the Appendix that corresponds to your fabric's width. Each square on these graphs equals 3". See page 142.

Consider Yardage Exceptions

In most cases, by completing the previous measuring and layout exercises you will accurately determine the required yardage for your slipcover. However, there are some exceptions (aren't there always exceptions to every rule!?):

Welting

If making welting from the shell fabric, add one extra yard to your overall yardage requirements for a chair slipcover. For a larger project or multiple projects, like a sofa, a pair of chairs and accent cushions, add 1½ to 2 yards.

Fabrics with Nap or Distinct Weaves

If your fabric has a nap, a distinct vertical or horizontal weave or an obvious "up" and "down," you may be restricted to the straight grain layout, which typically requires more yardage. This was the case for the tutorial chair's fabric, which has a horizontal weave.

Print Fabric

If your fabric has noticeable, repeating motifs, you must determine how much extra yardage you will need to position these motifs and match them, when possible. Here's what you need to know about printed fabrics in order to make these calculations.

Print Analysis

Printed fabrics and other fabrics with large woven designs have *repeats,* defined as the vertical and/or horizontal repetitions of motifs. You must identify the pattern of repeating motifs and plan your slipcover project around it.

There are two types of fabric repeats: *straight* and *half-drop*. Some textile manufacturers may include repeat information on a fabric label, noting increments of horizontal repeats across the fabric width and increments of vertical repeats down the fabric length.

Some of these prints are directional, too, meaning there's an obvious "up" and "down" to the pattern. Check the fabric's selvage: The print direction is usually noted with an arrow indicating "up."

If this information is absent on the fabric label or selvage, you're on your own to figure out the repeats. Do not hesitate to ask the sales clerk to unroll several yards for your inspection. Take your time studying the print and use the photos on the next page as a guide.

Straight Repeat

Half-Drop

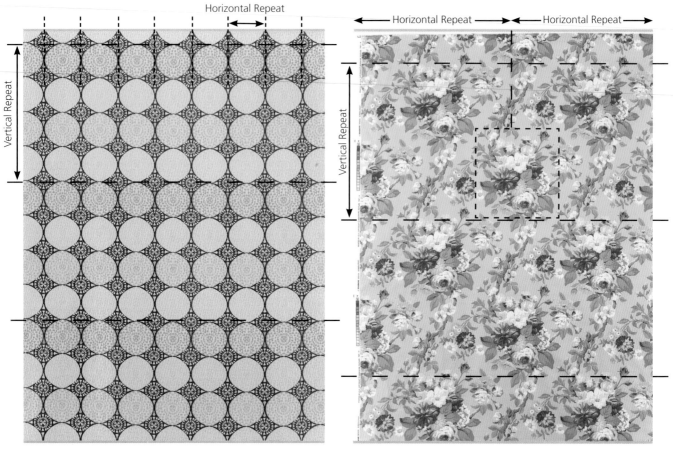

This jacquard fabric has a straight repeat. Think of each horizontal row of "dots" as a stripe, with the most prominent dot color being gold. Let your eye travel down four rows (gold, light gold, taupe, off-white). At the fifth row, the pattern repeats. This is the vertical repeat, which measures 17½" Move your eye across the fabric width—in each horizontal row of same-colored dots, the dot repeats every 3¾". This is the horizontal repeat.

This floral print has a "half-drop" of repeating primary motifs (the primary motif is outlined). Let your eye travel down the fabric length at one selvage edge. The primary motif repeats every 27"; this is the vertical repeat. Now, let your eye travel across the fabric width within the vertical repeat area … there are two parallel motifs, plus another motif located diagonally down and centered between them. This diagonal repeat, which occurs at the mid-point of the full vertical repeat, is what makes this print a "half-drop."

Print Positioning and Yardage Requirements

The focal points of a chair slipcover are primarily the seat or deck and the inside back (or the cushions that cover them). Concentrate on these areas as you plan the flow of pattern on your chair. With a straight repeat, you may be able to "connect the dots," so to speak, by lining up the pattern so that as your eye moves horizontally across or vertically down your slipcover project to appear seamless.

However, with a half-drop pattern, it's unlikely that you'll be able to match the pattern "seamlessly" around the chair's interior. So, do your best to position the primary motif in the center of the seat cushion (or deck), in the center of the back cushion (or inside back), and, if possible, in the center of the inside and outside arms, too.

If using a large-scale print, I recommend that you lightly mark your layout graph with repeat intervals and the points within the repeat areas where the primary motif appears. Then, as you graph the layout, you can position panels so that motif(s) are centered in them. Sometimes a half-drop pattern will allow for an extra cut within a full vertical repeat, but don't count on this. Error on the side of more yards (not fewer). You can always use leftover fabric to make arm covers, decorative pillows or a new seat cover for an accessory chair, like the one shown below.

A 20" x 20" panel of leftover fabric (primary motif centered) and a staple gun were all it took to recover the drop-in seat of this desk chair…a nice companion to the floral love seat shown below.

Below left: I was able to match this fabric's straight repeat so that the vertical rows of "dots" flow without interruption from the back bolster cushions, down and across the seat cushion to its front box band. Note: The fabric on these cushions is railroaded (to avoid seams). Below right: The half-drop floral pattern was too hard to match around the inside of this love seat, so I centered the primary motif on the inside back panels and seat cushions.

Determine Yardage of Other Materials
Cording Yardage

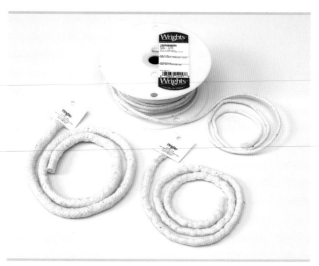

I recommend that you welt your slipcover seams for esthetic and practical reasons. Welting is a classy detail that naturally draws the eye to the shapely elements of a piece of furniture. Because welting is raised and located at stressful seams, it takes more of the wear and tear of use over time, thus preserving larger areas of fabric. During construction, you'll find that welting creates nice, wrinkle-free edges and corners (that otherwise would be hard to press). It also creates a uniform look even if your corner-cutting and position-basting haven't been exactly perfect. Welting is a very forgiving edge accent!

Some manufacturers call their cording "welt cord"; other calls it "piping cord" or "piping filler cord." Avoid very stiff, non-pliable cording (made from tightly twisted fibers or even plastic). This cording is appropriate for very heavy upholstery fabric, as well as vinyl and leather. Instead, look for softer cotton cording that's either twisted or made from loose batting material encased in mesh (my personal preference).

The latter cording is available in several common dimensions. The smallest is $^6/_{32}$" and is similar in size to most upholstery welting; it creates a traditional look. For more noticeable accent welting, you may decide to use the $^{12}/_{32}$" size. Reserve the $^{18}/_{32}$" and larger sizes for creating hem accents.

To determine your cording yardage for welting, measure the edges of the detached cushion(s), the chair perimeter (the No. 7 measurement; see page 26), and other welted edges of the underlying upholstery that you've decided to repeat in your slipcover. Combine these measurements and add one extra yard. The resulting figure is your cording yardage.

Pliable and soft, mesh-encased cording is an excellent choice for slipcovers. Pictured (clockwise, starting at the top) are: $^6/_{32}$" cording; $^{12}/_{32}$" cording; and $^{18}/_{32}$" cording.

Zipper Chain Yardage

Measure the lengths of the existing zippers in the detached cushions. Also measure the back right vertical edge of your chair from its upper edge to the floor. Combine these measurements (adding about 3" to 4" extra) to determine the required zipper chain yardage. Purchase one pull/stop set for each cushion cover and one more set for the shell's zipper closure.

Metal zipper chain is both economical and practical. You can buy exactly what you need and cut it into custom lengths. Because it's metal, this zipper can be fused (with fusible hem tape) over the basted insertion seam, thus eliminating awkward and inaccurate zipper pinning.

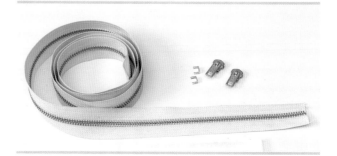

Pre-Clean and Pre-Cut Your Fabric

Pre-clean:

To avoid future shrinkage issues, follow the manufacturer's instructions to wash or dry clean your fabric before you cut it.

Pre-cut:

Refer to your cutting charts and sample layout to cut the following panels in their determined dimensions:

- Fabric yardage for welting (if made from the slipcover fabric); cut this yardage first and set it aside.

- Inside back, inside arm, arm front, deck, outside arm and outside back panels (except as noted at right).

- Box-edge cushion top and bottom panels

Cutting Exceptions:

- Skirt Panels: Do not cut the skirt panels until you review the instructions beginning on page 72 in Chapter 5 so that you can plan panel cuts that result in less conspicuous joining seams.

- *Box-Band Panels:* Do not cut the box-band panels for box-edge cushion covers until you review the instructions beginning on page 45 in Chapter 3. You will cut a separate zipper panel in a unique dimension.

- *Mock-Box, Knife-Edge and Bolster Cushion Panels:* Do not cut these cushion panels until you have reviewed the instructions beginning on page 49 in Chapter 3.

- *Inside and Outside Arm Panels and Inside Back Panel:* Do not cut these panels if your chair has curved or sloping arms until you have reviewed the instructions beginning on page 94 in Chapter 6.

Chapter 3

Making Welting; Making Cushion Covers

Mid-century "modern" is back—big time—in trendy contemporary interiors. These '60s-something daybeds were a blast from the past that needed some TLC for a 21st century revival. Their new cushion interiors and new cushion covers are projects that amply illustrate the techniques discussed in this chapter.

Revive Your Cushions

Sometimes a chair, or other furniture piece, is literally all cushions. This is the case with these daybeds that feature loose bolsters and large seat cushions (a.k.a. mini mattresses) that sit low to the ground on teak frames. For these companion couches, the slipcover process began and ended with new foam and batting interiors encased in outer covers sewn in this old/new geometric jacquard.

We found these mid-century masterpieces at an estate sale about 15 years ago, and they went straight to the basement rec room. I initially recovered them in a sturdy striped canvas, which lasted through years of slumber parties and other teen gatherings. When it was time for our son to move into his first bachelor pad, he asked to take these daybeds with him, and like any good mother, I gave them a fresh look and feel with new interiors, built from scratch, and new covers sewn in this contemporary fabric. Other vintage finds from the '50s and '60s (the coffee table, end table and lamp) fit right it for a retro-metro look. Cool, huh?

A similar cushion revival may be required for your slipcover project if the existing cushions are just too pooped to plump.

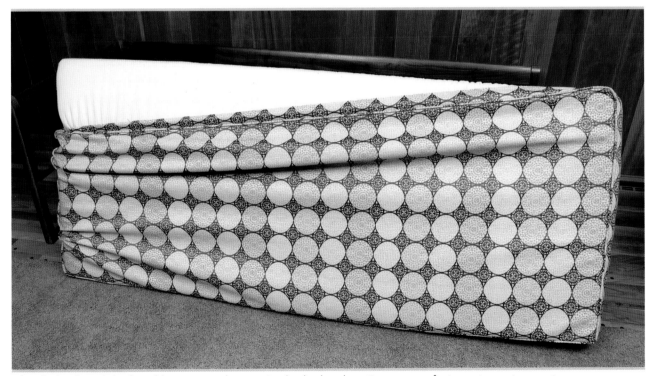

The daybed's original cushions were shot, so I asked a local mattress manufacturer to custom-cut two 72½" x 24" x 5" slabs of high density foam, which I wrapped in high-loft quilt batting and encased in muslin covers. What an improvement over the old sagging seats!

Make New Inner Cushions
(as necessary)

You've tested your chair's loose cushions—and they don't pass muster. It's time to build new ones. Here's how:

● **Materials**

High density upholstery foam in the dimensions of the original cushion

Quilt batting (high-loft for a softer cushion; low-loft for a firmer cushion)

Muslin (to cover the foam)

Electric carving knife

● **Instructions**

1 Shop for high density upholstery foam in fabric stores, at upholstery shops or workroom, or at a local mattress manufacturer, which is where I purchased the foam used in the daybed seat cushions shown on the previous pages. You can also look online. Type in "upholstery foam" or "upholstery supplies" in your search engine to find an online vendor.

2 If making several cushions, it may be economical to purchase a foam slab in the required depth and cut it yourself. To cut the foam, mark the cushion's length and width with a fabric marker. Place the foam on your cutting table with one marked line aligned with the surface edge and the foam extending beyond it. Lightly depress the foam on the marked line with a yardstick and cut the edge with an electric carving knife. Repeat to cut all sides. Do your best to make perpendicular cuts to maintain square corners and edges.

3 Wrap the cut foam in one or more layers of quilt batting and trim the batting at one foam edge. Use a needle and thread to whipstitch the batting edges with long hand stitches.

4 From muslin, cut one top and one bottom panel that are each 1" wider and 1" longer than the foam slab (minus batting). Also, cut and piece, as necessary a band panel that is 1" deeper and 1" longer than the foam depth and slab perimeter, respectively.

5 Refer the instructions given in Construct a Box-Edge Cushion, beginning on page 47, to assemble the cushion's muslin cover. Leave one muslin cover edge unstitched for cushion insertion.

6 Insert the cushion in the muslin cover. Fold under the ½" seam allowances on the open muslin edges, and whipstitch them together. The cushion is now ready for its new cover.

Layer It On!

Cushion making calls for several layers, but they are all important. The muslin protects the batting which might otherwise stick to the outer fabric and shift, creating unsightly lumps and bumps. The batting protects the foam, which could break down if it rubs against the wrong side of the cover fabric. Batting also softens the foam and its edges so the finished cushion doesn't end up looking like a brick.

Make the Welting

Your first task is to make all of the welting you will need for your project, plus one extra yard. Why? Even though welting is not hard to make, it is a multi-step process that will slow you down if you run out at a crucial point. ("Running out" is a moment of primal screaming that all sewers have experienced at one time or another.) Don't let this happen to you! Take a deep breath, plug in your IPod® or tune into reruns of *Law & Order*. In less than two episodes, your welting will be done!

● Instructions

1 Refer to the chart on the opposite page to determine the required width of the bias strips to cover your chosen cording.

2 *Note:* If your cording size is not listed, you can determine the bias strip cut width by wrapping a tape measure around the cording and pinching the tape at the cording edge. This measurement is the cord circumference. Add 1" to the cord circumference for seam allowances; the resulting measurement is the cut width of the bias strip.

3 I recommend that you not cut or use bias strips that are less than 6" long. Why? Welting made from short strips requires frequent seams and looks choppy. I also recommend that you intersperse shorter strips amid longer ones, so the joining seams will be staggered.

4 Follow the steps on the following page to cut the welting fabric into bias strips, and assemble the strips into a continuous length of bias.

● Materials

Welting fabric: approximately 1 yd. for a chair project; 1½ to 2 yards for a larger project

Cording in selected size and determined yardage

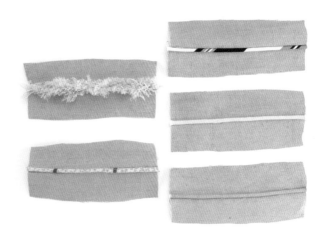

Making all of your welting up-front is a practical and time-saving endeavor.

Bias Strip Yields
From 1 Yard of 54"-wide Fabric

Cording Size (approx. diameter)	Bias Strip Width	Yield
$^{6}/_{32}$"	$1\frac{1}{2}$"	About 40 yd.
$^{12}/_{32}$"	$1\frac{3}{4}$"	About 30 yd.
$^{18}/_{32}$"	2"	About 20 yd.

Fold the welting fabric diagonally across its width and finger-press the crease. Cut the fabric into two sections on the crease line. Use a yardstick and fabric marker to mark the strip cutting lines in the desired width. Cut the strips on the marked lines.

Stack the cut strips, mixing shorter strips amidst longer ones. Stitch two strips end-to-end in a diagonal seam. Repeat to assemble all strips into a continuous length of bias. Press the seam open and trim, as shown.

Place the continuous bias and cording in separate piles underneath your work table. Starting at their cut ends, wrap the bias strip, wrong-sides together, around the cording, and use your zipper foot to baste the raw edges in a ½" seam until your piles are all used up!

Before and After: Plain cording is transformed into welting that's ready to be inserted into the seams of your slipcover project.

Construct a Basic Box-Edge Cushion Cover

Making the cushion covers at this point is not essential—in fact, you could make them later. However, the psychological benefit of making them now is "priceless." Once you see how beautiful your new cushions look, you'll be spurred on to complete the shell!

If making more than one cushion cover, be sure to "bundle" certain tasks, such as cutting multiple box-band panels, preparing and inserting multiple zippers. Trust me, bundling will reduce your construction time and improve the quality and consistency of your workmanship. Now, retrieve the previously cut top and bottom panels and the fabric reserved for the box bands. It's time to put them together!

● Materials

Top and bottom cushion panels previously cut in determined dimensions

Box-band panels cut in dimensions determined in step 2 below

Zipper chain in previously determined length, plus pull(s) and stop(s)

Pre-made welting

Fusible-web seam tape

The seat and back covers of the featured chair zipped off to reveal down-filled cushions in excellent condition. No need for new inner cushions here! These were ready for their new outer attire.

● Instructions

1 Skip these instructions if your original cushions are square or rectangular—the top and bottom panels you have cut are good-to-go and sew. However, for T-shaped cushions, you must trim the panels to mirror the cushion shape. To do this, place one cut panel right-side up and centered on the T-cushion, and trace the cushion outline. Remove the marked panel and add a ½" seam allowance beyond the traced line. Place this panel over its companion panel, wrong sides together, and cut both on the outer marked line.

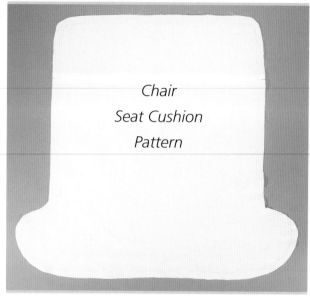

Chair
Seat Cushion
Pattern

Are you making multiple irregularly shaped cushion covers, such as the seat covers for these blue linen chairs and back cushions for the matching sofa? If so, I recommend creating muslin patterns, like these. Using a pattern ensures that all cut panels will be identical.

Sofa Back
Cushion Pattern

2 If you followed the cutting chart on page 28, you have reserved enough yardage to cut and piece two box-band panels that are 4" longer than the cushion perimeter and are 2" deeper than the cushion depth. Great! Now, you're ready to cut two specifically sized panels from your slipcover fabric.

- *For the zipper panel,* measure the length of the cushion's existing zipper, from pull to stopper. Add 2". This is the panel cut length. Add 2" to the cushion depth. This is the panel cut depth. Cut one panel in these dimensions.

- *For the remaining box band panel,* measure the remaining cushion perimeter from the zipper pull, around the cushion side, front, and side edges to the zipper stop; add 5" to this measurement. The resulting figure is the panel cut length. Add 1" to the cushion depth; this is the panel cut depth. Cut one panel in these dimensions.

3 Cut a length of zipper chain equal to the original zipper length. Slide the zipper pull onto the chain at one end, and pull it up and down the length of the zipper to synchronize the metal teeth. Attach the stop about ½" from the zipper's bottom edge.

4 Finish the zipper ends by encasing them in small fabric tabs with approximate ⅛" extensions, as shown in the photo below. Then, as you stitch across the zipper ends your needle will pierce the fabric extension, not the metal teeth—your sewing machine will thank you for this!

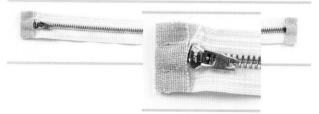

Encase the zipper ends in fabric tabs with slight extensions, as shown, and stitch in place.

5 Refer to following step-by-step photos to insert the zipper in its panel. (*Note:* These samples are mini versions of a full-scale zipper panel.)

A

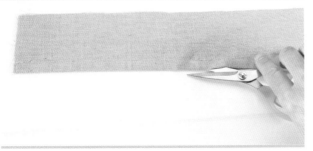

Fold the zipper panel in half, lengthwise and right-sides together; press the fold. Machine baste ½" from the fold as shown; create machine knots at both ends of the basted seam. Cut the panel in half on the foldline.

B

Open the panel and seam allowance and press flat. Center and fuse ⅞"-wide fusible-web seam tape over the basted seam allowance.

C

Fuse the zipper, right-side down over the seam. Stitch the zipper side edges and across its ends through the fabric tabs as shown.

6 Clip the basting stitches on the panel right side to open the seam and the zipper.

7 To assemble the box band, stitch the short ends of the zipper panel to the short ends of the box band panel in ½" seams. Fold the box band panel over the zipper panel ends to create 1"-deep pockets; baste the folds at the band edges to secure them. *Note:* The sample below depicts a very short zipper; your zipper will be much longer, of course.

Fold the excess panel over the zipper ends to create "pockets." Baste the panel edges to secure these folds.

8 Attach your zipper foot and, beginning at the back edge of one cushion panel, baste the welting around the panel edge. Refer to the step-by-step photos below to clip the welting at corners and to join the welting ends.

A

At each panel corner, clip the welting seam allowance and spread it to create a right angle. Baste around the corner, pivoting just above the clip.

B

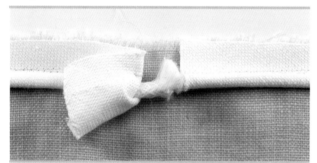

Stop basting about 3" from the welting beginning. Cut the welting end allowing about 2" more than you need to complete the welted edge. Open the welting casing end and trim out enough cording so that the cording ends butt together.

C

Turn under the excess casing fabric at the welting end and overlap the beginning. Baste over the welting "joint" several times to securely attach it to the panel.

9 To assemble the cover, pin-fit the box band around one top and bottom panels, centering the zipper panel on the panel back edge. Clip the band panel at the top/bottom panel corners for ease (like you did when basting the welting to the top/bottom panels). Also clip the band panel opposite edges at the same location (you will match these clips with the corners of the second panel). Stitch one panel to one band edge using your zipper foot.

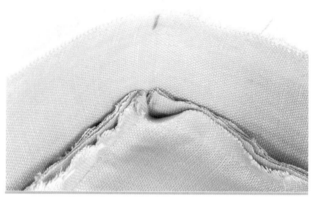

Above: Inside the cover, the stitched corners of the box band/cushion panels should resemble this assembly. Below: The welted edges of the outside corners should look like this.

10 Open the zipper half-way. Pin, then stitch the second panel to the opposite band edge, aligning the panel corners with the band clips. Trim the seams and corners, turn the cover right-side out through the zipper opening.

11 Insert the cushion and zip the cover closed. *Note:* To plump out the corners of your cover, stuff them with fiberfill before inserting the cushion.

Make a Mock-Box Cushion Cover

There's an alternative to the traditional box-edge cushion—the mock-box—pictured here as the back cushion on this blue linen chair. The upper and lower corners of this cushion may look a bit different, but they are created with the same technique.

You can change a chair's cushion covers from box-edge to mock-box, which is an easy-to-make treatment that eliminates the need for a separate box band. The seat back cushion of this chair is a mock-box style.

● Materials

Top and bottom panels cut in the dimensions determined in step 1

Zipper chain in previously determined length plus zipper pull and stop

Pre-made welting

Fusible-web seam tape

● Instructions

1 To cut the top and bottom panels, measure the original cushion's length, width and depth. Use these measurements to cut two panels in the following dimensions: (length + depth + 1") x (width + depth + 1".) *Example:* For a cushion that measures 24" x 20" x 3", you would cut two panels measuring: (24" + 3" + 1") x (20" + 3" + 1")...or...28" x 24".

2 Follow the step-by-step photos on page 50 to form corner darts on both panels.

A

At each panel corner, measure one-half the cushion depth plus ½" and mark.

B

Fold the panel corner diagonally to match the marks, then stitch each dart as shown.

C

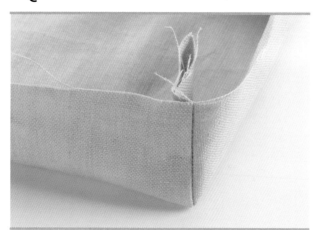

Turned right-side out, the dart creates a square corner. Neat!

3 On one panel, baste welting around the side-upper-side edges; leave the panel's bottom edge unwelted. To reduce bulk in seams, open the welting casings within the seam allowances at the panel lower edges and clip out the cording.

4 Follow the zipper insertion instructions beginning on page 41 to baste the panel lower edges and insert the zipper. Clip the basting stitches to open the seam and zipper.

5 Stitch the remaining panel edges; trim seams and corners. Turn the cover right-side out through the zipper opening. Insert the cushion and zip the cover closed.

The upper welted corners of a mock-box cushion cover look like this (above). The lower corners (below) may appear to be different from the upper corners, but they are created with the same mock-box technique.

Should You Remove the Existing Cushion Covers?

Loose cushions on upholstered furniture often have zippered, removable covers. You can dress these cushions in new covers placed over the old ones—many people, in fact, do this. I prefer to remove the original covers (if possible), because I don't like the look of welted edges on top of welted edges—double bumps, so to speak. You decide. If you keep the existing covers, you may need to sew slightly smaller seams to prevent a too-tight fit. Conversely, without the underlying covers, your new covers might need slightly larger seam allowances.

Make a Knife-Edge Cushion Cover

The knife-edge pillow is a mainstay in just about every décor setting. It fills empty spaces on all types of chairs, sofas and beds, and is by far the easiest cushion cover to make.

● Materials

Two panels cut in the dimensions determined in step 1

Zipper chain measuring 2" less than the length of the pillow edge where it will be inserted; zipper pull and stop

Fusible-web seam tape

● Instructions

1 Cut two panels 1" wider and 1" longer than the cushion. Baste two edges together and insert the zipper, referring to the instructions on page 46. Open the zipper seam and the zipper partway.

2 Stitch the remaining panel edges. Trim seams, clip corners and turn the cover right-side out through the zipper opening. Insert the cushion and zip the cover closed.

Seams Interesting

When sewing fabric with a nap, like faux suede, make sure to stitch in the direction of the nap. Otherwise, the nap may fight you (and your machine) and cause the layers to shift, resulting in uneven seams.

Instead of one-piece panels, make each from four squares like the faux suede floor pillows shown above.

- To determine the cut size of each square, divide each of the cover's finished dimensions by two and add 1". Example: If the cover's finished dimensions are 24" x 24", cut four 13" x 13" squares for each cover side (24" ÷ 2 = 12"; 12" + 1" = 13").

- Piece the squares, making sure your piecing seams crisscross exactly, and then follow the previous instructions to complete the cover.

Tips for Sewing Any Welted Seam

- For firm not "flabby" welting, let your zipper foot ride slightly over the welting edge and stitch the seam just inside the welting basting. If you can see the basted stitches on the cover's right side, your seam isn't tight enough—stitch it again!

- Although placing pins perpendicular to the fabric edge is the customary method used in garment making, it's just not practical for stitching welted seams. Pin vertically over the welting basting stitches, making sure the pin heads are toward you. They will be easier to remove as you sew the seam.

- When stitching any seam, do not stitch over pins—you can break your needle, the pin, the thread (or all three) and create burrs and scratches on your machine's feed dogs. Remove each pin as you come to it.

Make a Bolster Pillow Cover

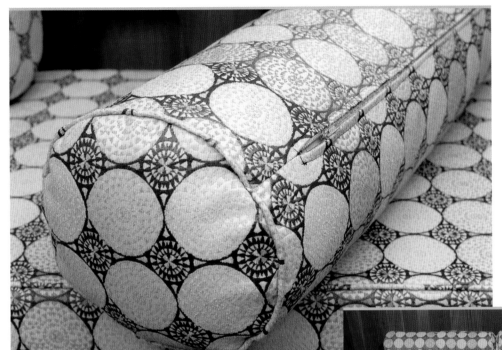

Out with the old wedges that previously populated the daybed backs—and in with round bolsters. These replacement pillows covers are easy to make.

● Materials

Purchased bolster cushion

Fabric panels cut in the determined dimensions. *Note:* Yardage will depend on the size of your cushion. The featured pillow measures 36" x 18" and has a 36" circumference. Each cover required 1⅛ yd. of 54"-wide fabric.

Zipper chain that measures about 6" less than the bolster length, plus zipper pull and stop

Pre-made welting

Fusible-web seam tape

These daybeds originally had a row of wedge-shaped foam cushions (hard as rocks!) along their backs. I replaced them with bolster pillows that I found for $6 each in the clearance aisle of a discount retailer. All they needed were new covers to match the seat cushions. Follow this easy construction process to cover bolsters as replacements for the outdated (or uncomfortable) back cushions of your slipcover project.

The key to successfully joining curved and straight edges, such as the end and body panels of a bolster cover, is to adequately notch the curved seam and clip the straight one. The notches will reduce the bulk of the curved edge and the clips will spread the straight edge to help you avoided creating tucks and puckers as you sew the seam.

1 Measure the length and circumference of the bolster cushion and add 1" to each dimension; these measurements are the body panel cut width and length. Measure the diameter of the end panel and add 1" to this measurement; this measurement is the cut diameter of the circular end panel. *Note:* Check your cupboards for a plate, circular tray or charger that may be just the right size for tracing the end panel.

2 Cut one body panel and two circular end panels in the determined cutting dimensions.

3 Baste the body panel lengthwise edges to form a tube, and follow the zipper insertion instructions on page 47 to insert the zipper. Clip basting stitches to open the seam and the zipper.

4 Refer to the welting insertion instructions beginning on page 48 to baste welting around each end panel and join the welting ends. *Note:* Clip the welting seam allowance before basting so that the welting will curve more easily around the panel edge.

5 Staystitch each body tube end just inside the seam allowance. Clip the seam allowance at regular intervals. Cut notches in the seam allowances of the end panels at regular intervals. Pin and then stitch an end panel to each body tube edge, easing the straight and curved edges as you sew.

6 Turn the cover right-side out through the zipper opening, push out the end panel seams to curve these edges. Insert the bolster pillow cushion in the cover and zip the cover closed.

Chapter 4

Constructing the Slipcover Shell

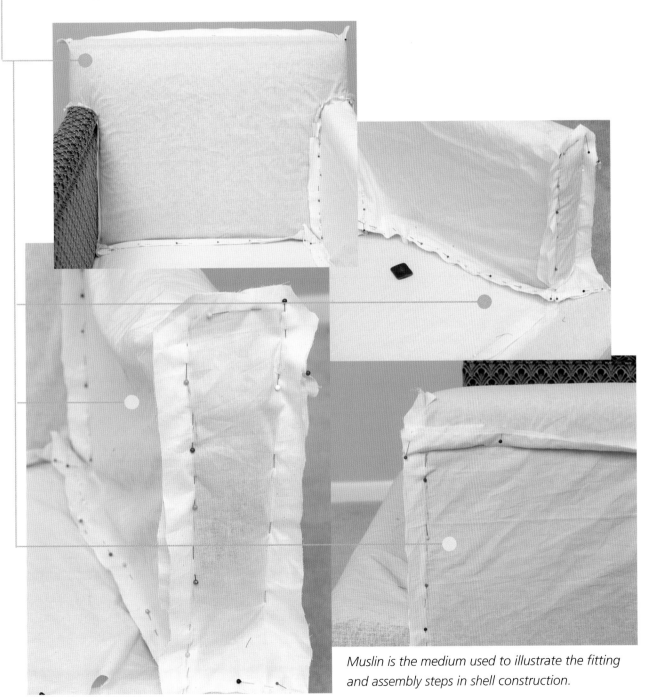

Muslin is the medium used to illustrate the fitting and assembly steps in shell construction.

The slipcover shell is where real fitting comes into play. You will work with some panels individually, and others in pairs as you pin-fit darts and tucks, and mark seam lines on the panels. Then, you'll take fitted sections—in stages—to your machine to stitch them. To facilitate this construction, either move the chair (or other furniture piece) to your sewing space, or move your sewing machine to the chair, as you will be going back and forth between them quite frequently.

Remember These General Instructions

In most of the following steps, you will place the referenced panel right-side down over its chair section. The panel cutting dimensions that you have determined and have noted in the chart on page 138 provide an extra 1" in width and length for fitting ease. Because of this, some seam allowances may be greater than ½" and/or uneven as you pin them together. (This is especially true for the outside arm panels, on a chair with a sloped back.)

Remember: You will first pin-fit the panels to the unique shape of the chair section and mark the seam lines. Then, you can trim the excess fabric to create uniform ½" seam allowances. After stitching the seams, clean finish them with pinking shears, machine zigzagging, or serging, as desired.

Note: The tutorial chair's slipcover features purchased cording (instead of fabric welting) in certain seams. It also has an upper arm treatment that mirrors the upholstery underneath—these seam and construction elements are unique to this chair.

Please use the following instructions as your benchmark for constructing the basic slipcover shell. After you have tried the basic method presented here, please feel free to digress and experiment with alternative constructions that you create "on the fly" (which is how I sometimes address some fitting issues). The unique characteristics of your furniture can only be addressed by you!

So, in the following discussions, just ignore the corded arm seams and follow my written instructions and the muslin samples.

General Construction Guidelines

- Place the panel right-side down on the furniture for fitting.

- Pin-fit first; mark seam lines second; trim excess fabric into uniform ½" seam allowances third.

- Stitch panels right-sides together in ½" seams.

- Clean finish seams as you stitch them by pinking, zigzagging, or serging, as desired.

Inside Back Panel

The inside back panel defines the shell structure. Pin-fitting, clipping and shaping this panel is your first task.

Shoulder Dart   *Inside Back Panel*

Pin each of the panel's "shoulder" darts and mark the dart stitching line. Also mark seam line on panel's outer edges where this panel will be joined (later) to the outside back panel. This seam is noted with a dotted line in the photo above.

Fit and Assemble the Inner Shell

Although muslin is used in the following step-by-step photos, you will be pin-fitting and marking the wrong side of the panels you have cut from your slipcover fabric.

● Instructions

1 Shell assembly begins with fitting the inside back panel. Center this panel, side-to-side and allow about 1" of excess fabric to extend beyond the chair's upper back edge. (*Remember:* The excess fabric at the panel's lower edge is the tuck-in allowance.) Secure this upper edge to the chair with T-pins.

2 To fit the chair's upper back corners (its shoulders), form darts from the excess fabric and mark the stitching lines. Feel for the chair's side, upper, then side back edges and mark them on the panel, as shown in the photo at left. This marked line will be your pinning and stitching guide when joining the inside and outside back panels (part of the outer shell assembly process explained later).

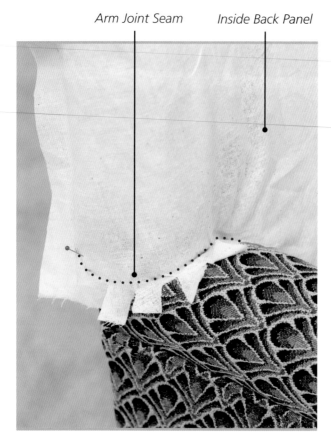

Arm Joint Seam   Inside Back Panel

Smooth the panel into/around each arm joint, making short clips initially and extending these clips as necessary to fit the fabric around the joint's curve. Be careful not to clip into the panel itself. Mark the arm joint stitching line with tailor's chalk.

3 Smooth the inside back panel into and around the inner curve of each arm where it intersects the chair back (the arm joint). Clip the fabric as necessary so that it lays flat around the curve. Starting at the outer back edge, mark each joint seam as shown. Leave this panel on the chair.

4 There are several ways to cut, fit and join inside arm and arm front panels, depending on the style of the arm, its underlying upholstery and your style preferences. The technique shown here is similar to the construction of a box-band cushion. Other arm fitting and construction techniques are presented in Chapter 6, beginning on page 87.

5 Are you adding welting around the arm front panel edges? If so, you must fit, mark and trim the arm front panels and baste welting around the panels' side, upper-side, then side edges.

To do this, place each arm front panel (right-side down and centered side-to-side) over the corresponding section of the chair. Allow about 1 " of this panel to extend beyond the uppermost point of the chair's arm front. Insert T-pins to secure these panels to the chair. Use tailor's chalk to trace the outline of the chair's arm front on each panel's wrong side.

Remove the marked arm front panels from the chair, and trim the excess panel fabric to an even ½ " beyond the traced lines. Baste welting around the arm panels' side, upper-side edges. Remember to open the welting casings within the panels' lower edge seam allowances and clip out the cording to eliminate bulk in future joining seams.

Arm Front Panel

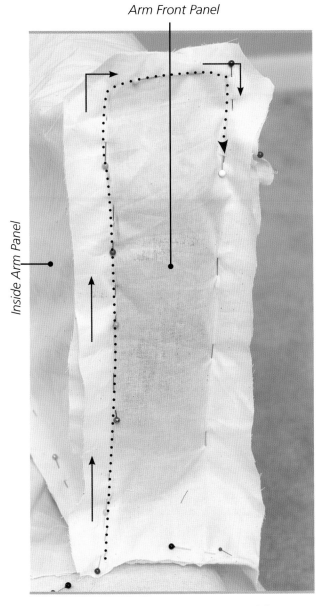

Inside Arm Panel

6 Place the plain (or welted) arm front panels over the chair's arm fronts and secure them with T-pins. Place an inside arm panel, right-side down, over each of the chair's inside arms; allow at least ½" of this panel's edge to extend beyond the front edges of the chair's arm.

Pin the front edge of each inside arm panel around the edges of its arm front panel. If working with an arm front with square upper corners, clip the corresponding seam allowances of the inside arm panel at these corners (just as you would if basting welting around a corner).

Mark the front-to-inside arm stitching line, as shown in the photo at left. Leave these pinned panels on the chair.

Pin-fit each arm front panel to the extended front edge of its corresponding inside arm panel. Clip the latter panel's seam allowance at the upper arm corners for ease (just as you would clip the seam allowance of a box band or welting if stitching either around a corner). To mark the stitching line, start at the inside lower edge of the arm front panel; mark up the length of this panel edge across its upper edge and then down to within ½" of the lower edge of the inside arm panel.

7 Now, it's time to clip and pin-fit the inside arm panels to the side edges of the inside back panel. To do this, fold back each inside arm panel's inner edge to mirror the shape of the arm joint. Clip the folded fabric for ease, just as you did when fitting the inside back panel around this joint. Starting at their lower deck edges, pin each inside arm to the inside back, and continue pinning up and around the arm joint and ending at the outside back. Mark the stitching line of each of these pinned seams.

8 Carefully remove the shell from the chair and take it to your machine. Stitch the shoulder darts. Next, stitch the inside back to the inside arms on the marked arm joint seams. Then stitch the arm fronts to inside arms along the marked seams, leaving the seam allowances at the ends of these latter seams unstitched.

Trim the seam allowances to a uniform ½" (as necessary) and clean finish them.

Place the partially assembled shell right-side down on the chair. Fold up and temporarily pin the tuck-in allowances of the arm front, inside back and inside arm panels so that they will be out of the way while you fit and construct the deck panel in the following steps.

9 The instructions given in the following steps address cutting, fitting and joining a T-shaped deck panel to the inner shell (i.e. stitching the deck around the arm front/inside arm/inside back/inside arm/arm front lower edges). If your chair has a rectangular deck with no T-extensions, see Alternate Deck Construction sidebar on page 67.

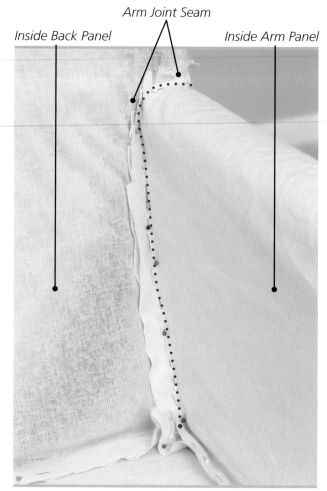

Inside Back Panel   *Arm Joint Seam*   *Inside Arm Panel*

Carefully pin the fitted inside arm to the fitted inside back along the curved arm joint; mark the stitching line.

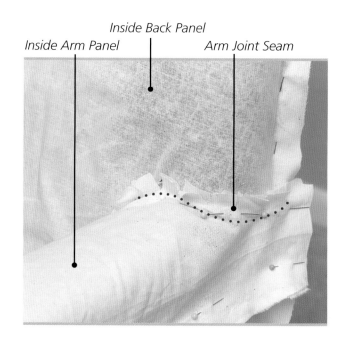

Inside Arm Panel   *Inside Back Panel*   *Arm Joint Seam*

10 A T-shaped deck panel consists of two separate panels constructed from the single pre-cut deck panel. *Note:* The previous measuring and cutting instructions take into consideration the potential of a joining seam, and the deck panel has been sized to allow for this.

11 To create these two deck panels, place the pre-cut deck panel, right-side down, on the chair deck. Center the panel side-to-side. Adjust the panel forward and backward so that the excess panel fabric flows over the deck front edge and 1" beyond the point where the skirt will be attached.

12 Fold the excess panel fabric at the front edge back and over the deck panel, making sure it has an even depth and that its fold is ½" forward from the inner corners of the T-crevices. Finger-press the fold; then, with the panel still on the chair, slit it into two sections on this fold. Set the smaller panel aside.

13 To trim and shape the larger deck panel, fold back the excess fabric at its side-back-side edges to conform to the shape of the chair's deck. Trim the excess fabric at the deck's side edges to a depth that is equal to the depth of the folded-back section on the deck's back edge. (*Note:* These folded-back sections are the deck tuck-in allowances.) Mark the side-edge folds at their front edges.

14 Retrieve the smaller deck panel and place it over the front edge of the deck as originally positioned. Pin the smaller and larger panels at their slit edges, beginning and ending this pinned seam between the folds marked in step 13, above. Mark the pinned seam.

15 Pin-fit the smaller deck panel's front corners with darts and mark the dart stitching lines.

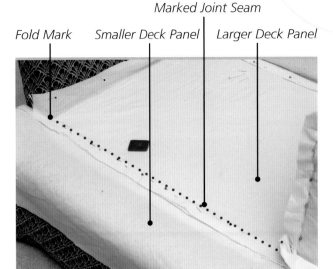

Fold Mark   Smaller Deck Panel   Marked Joint Seam   Larger Deck Panel

Pin the slit edge of the smaller deck panel to the slit edge of the larger deck panel as shown and mark the stitching line.

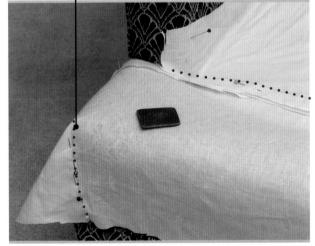

Dart Stitching Line

At the front corners of the deck T extensions, fold the excess deck fabric into darts and pin them. Mark the dart stitching lines.

16 Carefully remove the pinned deck panels from the chair, and stitch their joining seam and the front corner darts. Place the assembled deck panel on the chair, right-side down.

17 Now, it's time to stitch the fitted deck to the inner shell. First, remove the pins that are holding the inside-arm and inside-back tuck-in allowances out of the way (see step 8 on page 60). Clip the seam allowance of the larger deck section at each end of the deck joining seam. These clips will release the fabric and allow it to be pinned to the inner shell edges that are perpendicular to it.

Beginning and ending at these clip marks, pin the edges of the larger deck section to the corresponding inner shell edges, matching the deck back edge corners with inner shell seams; mark the stitching line. *Note:* You may experience some easing issues when pinning these edges. Don't worry! A tuck here or there will not matter as the seam you are pinning will be concealed within the chair's deck crevice.

18 Next, pin the raw edge of the smaller deck (the edge that extends across the T-extension) to the lower edge of the arm front panel, folding up the excess arm front fabric as shown in the photo at left. *Note:* This small fold of excess fabric becomes the tuck-in "pocket" at the T-crevice when the shell is turned right-side out.

Larger Deck Panel *Inside Arm Panel*

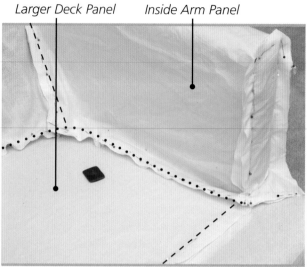

Clip the larger deck seam allowances at each end of the deck joining seam, and pin its side-back-side edges to the inside arm-inside back-inside arm lower edges, as shown. Mark the stitching line around these three edges.

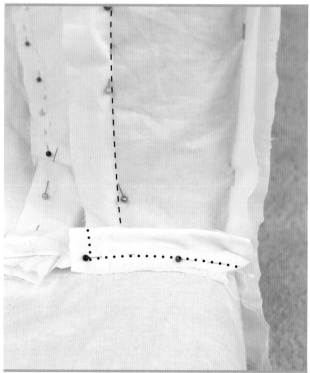

Starting at the clips made in the larger deck section's seam allowance, pin the edge of the smaller deck section to the lower edge of each arm front panel. Fold up the excess arm front panel fabric as shown.

19 Carefully remove the pinned panels from the chair and stitch the three pinned seams, being careful not to catch the deck joining seam allowances and the arm front seam allowances in your stitches. Turn the inner shell right-side out and you will see that you've created the "pocket" that tucks into the T-crevice of the chair. The arm front edges at the interior corner of this pocket are open, however. Pin these edges, right-sides together, and stitch these openings closed.

Congratulations! You have finished the inner shell of your slipcover and tackled the two most difficult fitting and seaming tasks: the arm joints and the deck fitting. It wasn't all that hard, was it? Now, it's time to move on to the outer shell assembly.

Important outcomes of all your careful pinning, clipping, folding and stitching are smooth fitting arm joints (shown above) and small tuck-in pockets located between each arm front panel's lower edge and the inner edge of the T extension (shown left). These are the greatest fitting challenges of any slipcover— everything else will be easy by comparison!

Tuck-in Pockets

Alternate Deck Construction

Straight Deck

Many furniture pieces have what I call a "straight deck," that is, one that traverses in straight lines from the back corners of the deck to the front without any T-extensions. Fitting a straight deck is similar to fitting a T-shaped one—in fact, it's easier. The photo below illustrates the seam that joins a straight deck panel to the inside arm and inside back panels.

Arm Front Panel   Deck Panel

Inside Arm Panel   Inside Back Panel

The deck assembly here simply entailed pinning and then stitching the inside arm and inside back to the deck panel edges—no need to clip fabric or seam allowances to traverse the interior corner of a T extension.

Deck with Partial Tuck-in Crevice

You've felt around the deck of your furniture and the crevice stops 4" (more or less) from the deck front edge on each side. Hmmm, now what? The solution is easy. Cut the deck and inner arm panels as if the tuck-in crevice goes around the entire deck. Refer to the muslin mock-up pictured below to fold up the tuck-in allowances of the inner shell panels, then pin these panel edges to the deck panel as shown and mark the stitching line.

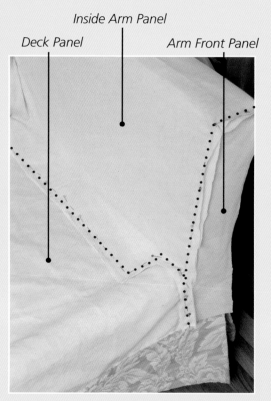

Inside Arm Panel

Deck Panel   Arm Front Panel

Pin the deck to the arm front and inner arm edges to fit the deck area without a crevice and mark the stitching line. Where the tuck-in crevice begins, pin the panels at a right angle— and another right angle—to create the tuck-in "pocket." Trim out the excess panel fabric before stitching the seam.

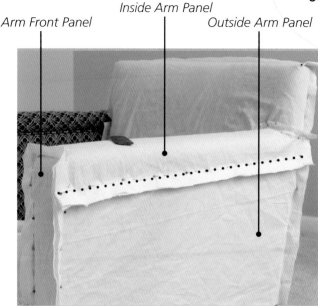

Arm Front Panel   *Inside Arm Panel*   *Outside Arm Panel*

Attach the Outer Shell

● Instructions

1 Place the assembled inner shell over the chair, right-side down.

2 Place the outside arm panels, right-side down, over the chair sections and secure them with T-pins. Pin-fit each outside arm panel to the inside arm and arm front edges, as shown. Make sure to align the horizontal inside and outside arm seam with the chair's underlying upholstery seam. Mark the seam lines. Carefully remove the pinned shell from the chair and stitch the marked seams separately, being careful not to stitch into the seam allowances of the adjacent seams.

3 Place the shell, right-side down, on the chair again.

4 Pin the outside back panel, right-side down, to your chair's outside back. Position this panel, side-to-side, to allow for at least a ¾" seam allowance along the left vertical edge of the chair (this edge will be where the zipper is inserted later). Feel for the chair back's side-upper-side edges and mark them on this panel (as you did when marking the outer edges of the inside back panel.

5 Remove this panel from the chair. Baste welting around its side, upper and side edges on the traced lines. Open the welting casing in the lower edge seam allowances and clip out the cording to remove bulk in the future skirt joining seam.

Pin-fit two edges of the outside arm panel to the inside arm horizontal edge (above) and the arm front vertical edge (below).

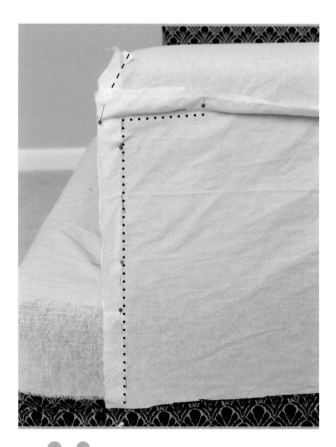

6 Place the welted outside back panel, right-side down, over the chair outside back. Pin the outside back panel side and upper edges to the outside arm and inside back edges, as shown. *Note:* If your chair has a slanted back, the seam allowances and excess fabric of the outside arm panels will increase as you pin the vertical seams. Just trim this excess fabric off.

7 Remove the cover and stitch the outside back right vertical edge, upper horizontal edge, and about 2" of the left vertical edge in one continuous seam, pivoting at the shoulder corners. Leave the remaining left vertical edge open for zipper insertion later. *Note:* When the shell is turned right-side out, the zipper opening will be along the right back edge of the chair.

8 Turn the shell right-side out and place it on the chair. Push the excess deck fabric into the chair deck crevices. Address any fitting issues (too tight, too loose) by taking in or letting out seams, as necessary.

Congrats, again! You've just finished the slipcover shell.

Pin the outside back panel to the shell edges. Mark the seam line and trim off some of the excess fabric, but leave at least ¾" beyond the marked seam line at the left vertical edge (the zipper seam).

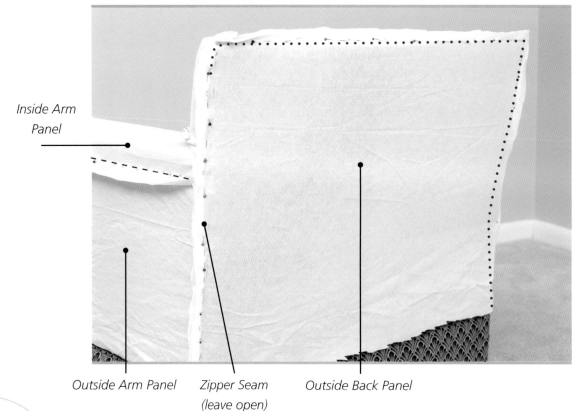

Inside Arm Panel

Outside Arm Panel *Zipper Seam (leave open)* *Outside Back Panel*

Chapter 5

Adding the Skirt and Creating Closures

Skirts and closures: Add pizzazz to your slipcover project with plentiful pleats, neat edge treatments, and some different closure options.

Learn the Basics and Go Beyond

The shell is done. Now, let's move on to the skirt and the shell closure. The initial instructions in this chapter address cutting, assembling, and attaching a skirt that is finished with a simple topstitched hem, and creating the traditional zipper closure. These techniques are illustrated in the tutorial chair's slipcover.

You may decide, however, to finish your skirt with a different edge treatment—scallops, welting or a band. And, you may choose an alternative closure, such as laces, buttons, or snaps. These alternatives are easy to make and won't affect the overall yardage requirements of your project.

But first, let's start with the basic skirt assembly. Instructions begin on the opposite page.

The tutorial chair's skirt features a simple topstitched hem and zipper closure along the back right edge.

Instead of a zipper, this patchwork slipcover gets its closure from a row of snaps down the center of its outside back panel.

Cut and Assemble the Skirt Panels
Review the Basics

Go back to Chapter 2 and review the information in Determine Skirt Panel Cutting Dimensions on page 29. You have already decided on your skirt style and have made the necessary calculations to determine the following:

- You have determined the panel *cut length* (the skirt finished length + 4½").
- You have determined the *number of panels* needed to create the skirt.

I've asked you to wait until now to actually cut the skirt panels because I want you to plan *their cuts* so that the joining seams will be either concealed inside pleats or, in the case of a flat skirt, positioned at the back corner(s) of the chair (or other furniture) where they will be less noticeable.

Note: In the following instructions, the chair's left and right sides are identified as if viewing the chair from the back. The right back vertical seam of the shell skirt is where you will insert the zipper closure.

Determine Panel Cuts

● Instructions

1 To determine the panel cutting dimensions of a flat skirt: Measure the outside back width of the chair where the skirt will be joined to the shell and add 1¼". Measure the remaining chair perimeter where the skirt will be attached (its side-front-side edges). Add 1¼" to this measurement. Cut two skirt panels in these determined widths x the determined cut length (which is, again, the finished skirt length + 4¼").

2 To determine the panel cutting dimensions of a skirt with corner pleats:
- Measure the chair width at each side where the skirt will be attached—back, left, front, right—and record these measurements.
- For the back and right-side panel cut widths, add one half of a single pleat allowance + 1¼" to the side measurement. Cut each panel in this determined cut width x the determined cut length.
- For the left and front panel cut widths, add 1" to their respective measurements. Cut each panel in this determined cut width x the determine cut length.
- For the pleat panel cut widths, add 1" to the single pleat allowance. Cut three pleat panels in this determined cut width x the determined cut length.

3 To determine the panel cutting dimensions of a gathered skirt: Just cut the determined number of panels in the determined cut length. The piecing seams will be concealed in the skirt gathers.

4 To determine the panel cutting dimensions of a fully pleated skirt: Get out your calculator! Too many variables (pleat depths, number of pleats, and so on) come into play; thus, setting forth a standard formula is more complicated than it's worth. Just remember to plan your panel cuts so that the joining seams are either on a pleat fold or concealed within a pleat.

Assemble the Skirt Panels

● Instructions

1 To assemble a flat skirt: Stitch the left short edge of the back panel to the right short edge of the long side-front-side panel in a ½" seam (this seam will align with the chair's back left edge). Press the seam open.

2 To assemble a corner-pleated skirt: Stitch the panel short edges, using ½" seams, in the following order, starting with the right panel: right panel, pleat panel, front panel, pleat panel, left panel, pleat panel, back panel. Press all seams open.

3 To assemble a gathered or fully pleated skirt: Join the panels, short edge-to-short edge, into one long flat panel and press the seams open.

4 Hem the panels: For all skirt styles, press under 2" twice on the panel lower edges and topstitch the hem close to the inner fold.

Form Gathers or Pleats

● Instructions

1 For a gathered skirt: Use your preferred method to gather the skirt upper edge to fit around the chair where the skirt will be attached. Allow ¾" of ungathered fabric at each open end for the zipper seam allowance.

2 For a corner-pleated skirt: Form three corner pleats to correspond with the chair's back left and two front corners. At the open ends (which will become part of the zipper seam when the skirt is attached to the slipcover shell), form half pleats as shown in the photos at right. Baste the upper edges of the pleats to secure them.

3 For a fully pleated skirt: Follow the instructions given for a corner-pleated skirt. Form full pleats around the skirt upper edge, and form half pleats at the open ends with ¾" seam allowances for the zipper seam (sewn later).

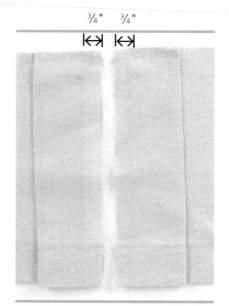

Box Half Pleats: Fold the skirt open ends into half box pleats; allow ¾" seam allowances for the zipper seam.

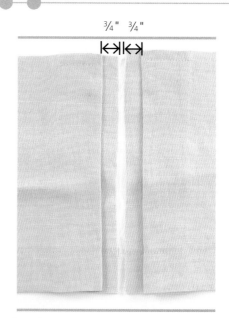

Inverted Half Pleats: Fold the skirt open ends into half inverted pleats as shown; allow ¾" seam allowances for the zipper seam.

Create Different Hem Edges

A topstitched hem is an easy way to finish a slipcover skirt. However, with a little extra sewing, you can jazz up your slipcover's ho-hum hem with welting, bands, scallops, and flanges.

Edgy! Contrasting welting at the hem adds subtle visual interest.

Welted Hem

Many years ago, my sister rescued this little chair from my grandfather's attic and covered it in a bright yellow cotton. It became my niece Emily's special reading chair. Today, Emily is an elementary school teacher. As a gift for the reading corner in her classroom, I rehabbed her old chair with a patchwork cover (that even has side pockets for books). One of its features is a welted hem. This is an easy edge treatment to replicate. Here's how:

● Instructions

1 After joining your skirt panels, trim 3½" from the skirt lower edge. Set this strip aside to use as the hem facing.

2 Baste contrasting welting around the skirt cut edge and join the welting ends, just as you would if basting welting around a cushion panel. Refer to the welting application instructions beginning on page 48.

3 Finish one long edge of the hem facing with a ½" topstitched hem. Stitch the facing around the skirt lower edge.

4 Press the facing up and inside the skirt and slipstitch it in place.

Accent Band

To edge your skirt with an accent band, follow the instructions below to adjust the cut length of your skirt panels. These instructions apply to accent bands cut either on the bias or cut on the straight grain. The seat cover shown in the photo features a bias-cut accent band made from the slipcover fabric.

● Instructions

1 The cut length of your skirt panels will depend on the desired finished width of the accent band. To determine the skirt panel cut length, use this formula:

skirt panel cut length =
skirt finished length – band finished width + 1"

2 Cut the required number of skirt panels in this determined cut length to accommodate your skirt style, and refer to the skirt assembly instructions on page 70 to join the panels.

3 To determine the band panel cut dimensions, use this formula:

band cut depth =
(band finished depth x 2) + 1"

band pieced length =
skirt lower edge circumference

4 Cut the band panels (on the bias or on the straight grain) in the determined cut depth so that, when joined end-to-end, their length equals the skirt circumference at its lower edge. *Note:* If cutting these band panels on the straight grain, plan their cut lengths so that their joining seams align with the skirt panel joining seams.

A stripe or a check fabric, cut on the bias, makes an interesting hem band. A contrasting solid also creates a sharp lower-edge accent.

5 Piece the band panels, end-to-end, to create the required band length. Press the seams open.

6 Press under ½" on one long band edge. Pin and then stitch the opposite band edge to the skirt lower edge. (See A at right).

7 Press the band-skirt seam toward the band. Fold the band in half, wrong-sides together, with the band folded edge slightly overlapping the band-skirt seam. Press the band outer fold.

8 Open the band. Apply fusible-web seam tape over the band-skirt seam allowance. Refold the band and fuse it to the seam allowance. (See B at right).

9 On the skirt-band right side, stitch in the ditch over the band-skirt seam to attach the band's self-facing to the skirt. (See C at right).

A

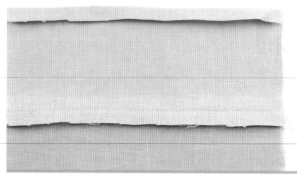

Press under ½" on one long band edge, and stitch the opposite long edge to the skirt lower edge.

B

Fuse the band folded edge to slightly overlap the band stitching line.

C

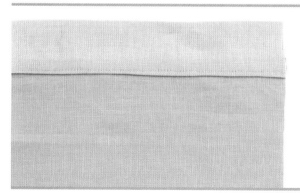

On the skirt right side, stitch in the ditch over the band-skirt seam.

Scalloped Hem

The only tool you will need to make this hem treatment is a large coffee or tea cup. Follow these instructions:

● Instructions

1 After joining the skirt panels, trim 3½" from the skirt lower edge. Set this strip aside for use as the hem facing.

2 Place the assembled skirt panels, right-side down, on a flat surface. Mark a ½" seam allowance along the skirt lower edge; mark a second parallel line 1¾" from the lower edge. Use a coffee or tea cup to trace the scallop shape on the skirt panel lower edge, as shown in A below.

3 Finish one long edge of the hem facing with a ½" topstitched hem. Pin the facing to the skirt panel lower edge right-sides together. Stitch the scallops on the traced line. Trim the excess fabric, cutting notches in the curves as shown. Turn the skirt and facing right-side out and press, as shown in B below.

This scalloped hem has universal appeal and can be used on many projects.

1

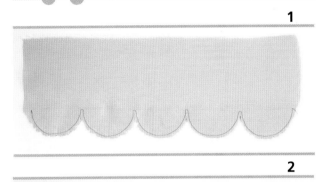

2

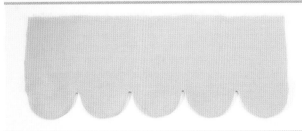

3

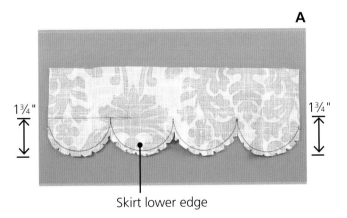

A

1¾"   1¾"

Skirt lower edge

Use a cup or other round object with its edge touching the marked ½" seam; trace its edge up to the second marked line. Move the cup left or right and repeat to trace the scallop shape around the entire skirt edge.

Stitch the scallop curves on the traced lines (black thread was ued to accentuate the stitching lines). Trim and notch the excess fabric (nos. 1 and 2). Turn the facing right-side out, push out and shape the scallops, and press (no. 3).

Flange Edges

I saw this detail in a high-end furniture store in Chicago. "Good heavens," I said to the sales clerk, "someone forgot to put cording in those welted edges!" The clerk politely informed me that the edges to which I referred were not welted. "They are *flanged*," he said. In my experience, a flange is a floppy edge found on bed pillow shams, but what the heck. This is one cute edge treatment that I used on the floral slipcover shown below. You can also add a flange to your skirt edge. Just follow these steps:

● Instructions

1 For flanged seams, first decide how wide you want the flange to be. To determine the width, experiment with a leftover bias strip from another project. Fold the bias in half width-wide, wrong-sides together. With raw edges aligned, baste the folded strip to the edge of a panel. Fold back the seam allowance and decide if you're satisfied with the width of the flange, then adjust the width of your bias strips accordingly. *Note:* I used 1½"-wide bias strips for the floral loveseat project shown. This bias produced a ¼" flange.

2 After deciding on the bias width, cut and join enough bias lengths to accommodate the desired seams of your slipcover cushions, shell and/or skirt edge.

3 Fold the bias strip in half lengthwise, wrong-sides together, and press the fold. The resulting bias strip is your flange. If using the flange as a seam accent, baste it into your seams just as you would if inserting welting.

4 If using flange at the skirt lower edge, refer to the Welted Hem instructions on page 72 to trim the excess skirt length and use it to make a hem facing.

5 Baste the flange around the skirt's lower edge. Considering pleating the flange at the skirt corners or at other intervals, forming three to five small knife pleats.

6 Finish one long edge of the hem facing with a ½" topstitched hem. Stitch the facing to the skirt. Press the facing up inside the skirt and slipstitch it in place.

Welting without the interior cording? It's the latest look called a "flange." It's an edge treatment you can use in the seams of cushions and the shell, and as a tasteful "trim" accent on your skirt, too.

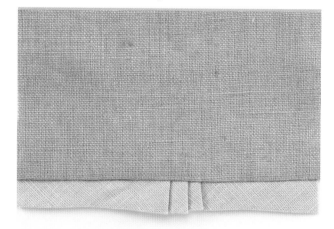

A flange with small knife pleats adds a nice crisp finish to a skirt hem.

Attach the Skirt to the Shell

The last step in Chapter 4 was to place your assembled shell, *right-side out,* on the chair and push the excess deck fabric into the deck crevices. In this position, your slipcover shell is now ready to accept its skirt. Here are two techniques for attaching the skirt to the shell.

Traditional Method

● Instructions

1 For all skirt styles, use a yardstick or hem marking tool to measure (from the floor up) the skirt finished length. Mark this placement line around the shell perimeter. Also mark the shell at the chair corners (for corner pleat placements). Trim excess fabric as necessary to create an even ½" seam allowance below the marked line.

2 Remove the shell from the chair and baste welting around the shell perimeter on the marked line. Open the casings at each end of the basted welting and trim out ¾" of cording.

3 Drape the shell lower edge over a flat surface (such as your cutting or work table). With right-sides together and raw edges aligned, pin the skirt upper edge over the basted welting, making sure to align the skirt pleats and seams with the corresponding shell corner seams and/or marked corners. Insert pins parallel and close to the welting inner edge.

4 Stitch the skirt to the shell, stitching slightly inside the welting basting stitches (just as you would stitch any other welted seam). Clean finish this seam.

My Alternative Method

● Instructions

1 Baste the welting to the skirt upper edge; open the casings at the ends of the basted welting and trim out ¾" of cording.

2 Fold under the welting seam allowance and pin the skirt upper edge around the shell, aligning the skirt pleats and seams with the chair corners, as applicable. By pinning the skirt's welted upper edge to the shell (as opposed to basting just the welting around the shell), you will be able to see exactly how the skirt looks and make any minor adjustments in its length and overall appearance before stitching it to the skirt.

3 After making any necessary adjustments, flip the skirt up and re-pin its upper welted edge to the shell, positioning your pins parallel and close to the welting.

4 Carefully remove the shell from the chair and take it to your sewing machine. Stitch the skirt to the shell slightly inside the welting basting stitches. *Note:* This is another advantage of this method … you will be able to see these basting stitches as you stitch the skirt to the shell.

5 Trim the shell-skirt seam allowance to an even ½" and clean-finish the seam.

Install the Zipper Closure

● Instructions

1 Pin and then baste the zipper seam on the previously marked stitching lines, being careful not to catch pleat folds and edges, if any, in this seam. Press the seam open.

2 Follow steps 3 and 4 on page 46 to finish the ends of the cut zipper chain with fabric tabs. *Remember:* This zipper will separate at its lower edge. Because of this, you must attach a separate fabric tab to each half of the zipper end at the zipper's lower edge.

3 Follow the zipper insertion instructions on page 47 to apply fusible-web seam tape to the seam allowance. Center the zipper over this seam so that it opens from the bottom up, and fuse it to the seam allowances.

4 You will stitch the zipper in two steps.
- First, on the shell inside, stitch the zipper edge that lays on the unwelted side of the seam. Start at the skirt lower edge, stitch up the length of the zipper and across the zipper upper edge. Make secure machine knots at the beginning and end of this stitch line.
- Second, on the shell outside, stitch in the ditch of the welting to secure the second zipper edge. Again, start at the skirt lower edge and stitch up the length of the zipper and across its upper edge to meet to previous stitch line.

5 Clip the basting stitches to open the seam and the zipper. Place the finished cover over the chair, right-side up, tuck in the excess deck fabric, and zip the cover closed. Place the newly covered cushions (if any) on the chair. Bravo! You've finished your first slipcover!

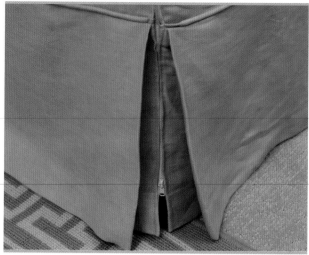

This chair's zipper closure fits nicely between the folds of an inverted corner pleat.

The zipper in this shell closure goes down the center of a corner box pleat.

Why a ¾" Zipper Seam?

The zipper seam for this slipcover joins the welted edges of the outside back and the welted upper edge of the skirt. This will be a bulky seam, even though you've trimmed out cording in the seam allowances. Bulk eats up seam allowances, so to be sure there's enough fabric in the seam to accommodate zipper insertion, I've added an extra ¼".

Make Different Closures

The traditional zipper closure is intended to work but is not meant to be seen (all that much). A center-back closure, however, showcases its functionality. This meant-to-be-seen closure requires two center-back panels, instead of one, with cutting dimensions determined below. These are minor cutting adjustments which should not change the overall yardage requirements of your project.

Emily's students will want to help her redress the class reading chair each time she launders it. This is why I chose sturdy, kid-friendly snaps for the closure.

It's a Snap!

● **Materials**

5 to 7 snaps

Snap setting tools or pliers

● **Instructions**

1 To make the snapped closure, cut two outside back panels in the following dimensions: cut width (one half the width of the chair outside back + 2½") x the determined cut length.

2 To create self facings, on each panel's inner vertical edge, press under ½" and then press under an additional 1½". Topstitch the facings close to their inner folds.

3 Lap the faced edges of outside back panels, left-over-right, and align their inner edges. Mark the desired number of evenly spaced snap positions, centered within the facing width, on both the upper and lower panels. *Note:* Make sure to position the lowermost snap at least 1" *above* the panels' lower edges.

4 Follow the manufacturer's instructions to install all snaps—except the lowermost snap—at the marked locations.

5 Snap the outside back sections together, and baste their upper and lower overlapped edges. For purposes of finishing the shell, treat these two sections as one panel.

6 To adapt the slipcover skirt for a center-back closure, you will cut the skirt panels in the determined cut length, but you must cut the skirt back panel into two sections. Follow the step 1 and step 2 instructions on page 79 to determine the cut width of each panel and finish the inner vertical edges of both panels with self facings.

7 Follow the instructions given in Attach the Skirt to the Slipcover Shell traditional method on page 77 to baste welting around the shell lower edge (extending the welting into the facings). Open the shell and skirt facings, and then pin and stitch the skirt to the shell.

8 To finish the closure, fold the facings inside the panels on their original fold lines, and slipstitch them in place. Install the final snap in its marked position.

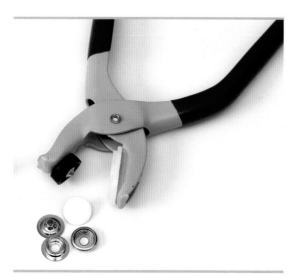

Button Me Up

A center-back button closure ahs the same construction as the snap closure. You will work horizontal buttonholes within the facing width to accommodate your chosen buttons. I used this closure because at one time this sofa was positioned as a room divider in a larger room, and its buttoned back was on full display!

A center-back button closure is a garment detail that may appeal to your inner couturier.

Snap hardware and setting pliers (left) are available at most fabric stores. Snap covers typically come in white, black and nickel. Choose a snap that works with your project and follow the manufacturer's instructions to install them at the marked locations, leaving the lowermost snap installation until after you have attached the skirt to the slipcover shell.

Lace Me Up

I admit, this laced closure is a bit over the top, but so is the fabric! This closure is also an option for less "girlie" projects, too. Think denim-covered headboard... in a boy's bedroom...with laced side closures! A cute look for a little cowboy, don't you think? Here's how to replicate this closure on your project.

● Materials

Suede lacing or other purchased cording

Eyelets or grommets with hole size to accommodate your chosen lacing material

Eyelet pliers or grommet setting tools

● Instructions

1 Complete the slipcover shell following the previous instructions with this modification: Allow 1" seam allowances in the zipper seam. Press under the seam allowances on both edges of the zipper seam.

2 Place the slipcover shell on a flat surface with the zipper seam folds butting. Mark the desired location of an even number of eyelets or grommets, evenly spaced, on each panel's right side. Position the eyelets directly across from each other and within the seam allowance area.

3 If your slipcover has a flat skirt, you may choose to lace the entire zipper seam. For slipcovers with fully pleated or gathered skirts, I recommend creating a closure for just the outside back and outside arm portion of the zipper seam. To finish the skirt open edges, press under the 1" seam allowance and topstitch side hems.

I substituted eyelets and suede lacing for the traditional zipper in this floral loveseat slipcover. The crisscrossed lacing reminds me of a lady's corset and seems in keeping with the lush print and overall feminine appeal of this project.

4 Follow the manufacturer's instructions to install the eyelets or grommets at the marked locations. Starting at the upper end of the closure, thread the lacing through the eyelet holes as if lacing up a shoe. Tie the lacing ends in a bow.

Chapter 6

Fitting, Slopes, Curves, Angles and More

In this chapter you'll learn how to custom fit the unique shapes and styles of larger furniture pieces, like sofas, as well as those with sloped and curved shapes.

Rolled, curved and sloped edges, plus asymmetrical sections may require fittings with extra seams, tucks and darts. Study your furniture's underlying upholstery details to determine whether to cut and join more than one slipcover panel to fit a particular section. Refer, also, to the fitting instructions given in this chapter as they relate to your furniture piece, and return to the general construction techniques presented in earlier chapters to complete your slipcover.

Make a Sofa Slipcover

Piece the Deck Inside Back and Outside Back

Although sofa slipcovers require more fabric, cording and welting, zipper chain, and so on, than their chair counterparts, their overall construction is the same with one exception: Because your sofa's length will be greater than the width of your fabric, you may have to cut and piece multiple panels for the deck, inside-back and outside back panels.

Piecing is a must if you're using a directional print with noticeable repeats or a fabric with a nap, both of which will require straight grain positioning on your sofa and a straight grain layout. (Review the Print Analysis information beginning on page 35 in Chapter 2.)

For a two-seat sofa, cut two panels per section with a center joining seam. For a three-seat sofa, you have two cutting-and-piecing options.

Option 1: Cut three panels of equal width and position their joining seams to flow between the seat and/or back cushions.

Option 2: Cut one center panel as wide as your fabric width and two smaller panels of equal width that, when joined, will cover these sections of the sofa.

This damask's directional half drop pattern required straight grain fabric placement on the sofa. Thus, I was required to cut and piece two panels each for the deck, inside back and outside back. I positioned the deck and inside back seams in the center (where they would be concealed between the loose seat and back cushions).

Railing the Deck, Inside Back and Outside Back

If, however, you are able to railroad the fabric on your sofa, you will be able to cut single panels for the deck, inside back and outside back, which, happily, was the case for this blue linen sofa slipcover.

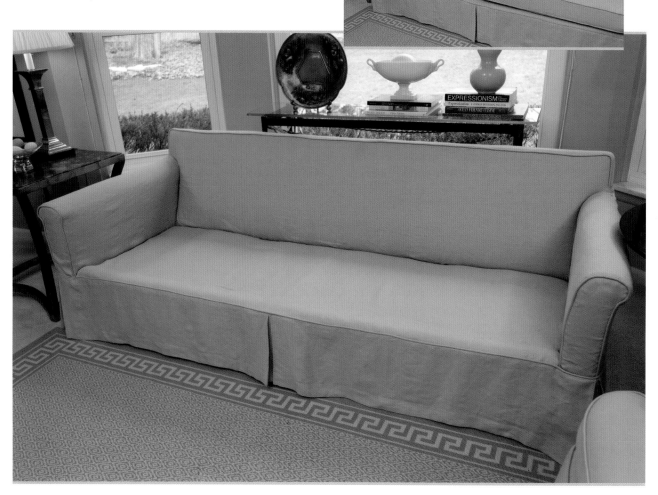

This linen fabric looks the same whether positioned on the straight grain or cross grain. Thus, I was able to railroad the fabric on the deck, inside-back and outside-back panels. I saved time by not having to cut and piece extra panels, and I saved money as railroading meant I needed fewer yards of fabric.

Yardage Conservation

Sofa decks just eat up fabric! And, if the fabric in question is expensive, you will feel the pain of using precious yardage under the seat cushions where it won't be seen by anyone, except, perhaps, a nosy guest. To conserve yardage (and control the cost of your project), take your cue from the custom slipcovers by some furniture retailers. Take a peek under the seat cushions. Ah ha! You may discover that a different fabric has been pieced into the center area of the deck.

You can use this yardage conservation technique, too. First determine the cutting dimensions of your deck panel. Then, use the formulas in the chart below to determine the cutting dimensions of an interior deck panel, cut from an alternate fabric, such as sailcloth or lightweight canvas, plus two side panels and one front panel, cut from the slipcover fabric. You can even create this interior panel, crazy quilt style, by piecing together odd-sized scraps of your slipcover fabric.

To assemble these panels, stitch the side panels to the interior panel's side edges and press the seams open. Stitch the front panel to the front edge of the side, interior, and press all the seams open.

Interior Deck Panel Cutting Dimensions
(cut one from alternate fabric)

width = determined deck panel cut width – tuck-in allowance – 10"
length = determined deck panel cut length – front overhang (if any)* – 5"

Deck Side Panel Cutting Dimensions
(cut two from slipcover fabric)

width = tuck-in allowance + 5½"
length = determined deck panel cut length

Deck Front Panel Cutting Dimensions
(cut one from slipcover fabric)

width = front overhang (if any)* + 5½"
length = determined deck panel cut width

*The "Front Overhang" equals the amount of fabric that extends over the deck's front edge to the point where the skirt is attached. Refer to the deck photo of the damask sofa on page 83; the front overhang on this slipcover measures 4". If your slipcover skirt is deck height, like the skirt of the blue linen sofa shown at left, there is no front overhang.

Should Your Slipcover Look Like Upholstery?

Furniture aficionados may disagree, but I say "no." Your mission is to create a cover that fits well, has nice details, and looks professionally made. Do not feel bad if your cover has a wrinkle or two or does not fit like a glove over certain curvaceous edges! This is part of the charm of slipcovers … they aren't supposed to be rigid replications of the underlying upholstery.

Consider, too, that you don't have access to the hidden areas of your sofa, chair, etc. (like upholsterers do), so you won't be able to pull some panels taut for an ultra-tight fit (using tacks or a staple gun is out of the question).

When you think about it, upholsterers have an easier time creating a good fit because all of their nips, tucks and staples edges are inside the furniture or concealed in crevices or under skirt panels. With the exception of tuck-in allowances, every seam of your work shows. And you should be proud of each and every one of them.

So, when someone points to your slipcovered piece and asks about its fabrication, you can reply with confidence and pride, "That's not ordinary upholstery, it's a custom slipcover. And I made it myself!"

No one would mistake these linen covers for upholstery, and that suits me just fine. I like the fabric's wrinkled appearance and the fact that the skirts brush the floor. It's a relaxed, more casual look that feels just right during the spring and summer months (the seasons of slipcovers in my living room).

Address Semi-Detached Back and/or Seat Cushions

This cute piece was abandoned by the previous owners of our first house. Poor little loveseat! We gave it a good home in our bedroom (with a new canary yellow slipcover), and later moved it to our daughter's room. Today, this loveseat wears a new slipcover and lives in the guest bedroom. In making this cover, I had to address this issue: What to do about the space between the semi-detached back cushions? Here are two potential remedies to consider if you encounter this feature in the back or seat area of your furniture.

- **Copy all of the upholstered details**. Think of a box-band cushion cover minus one panel—a half-box cover, of sorts. This is what you will construct to cover each semi-detached cushion. Make sure the depth of the band panels includes seam allowances to join them to each other and to the adjacent panels.

- **Ignore some or all of the details**. I didn't like the idea of double welting down the inside center back of my slipcover, so I stuffed batting in the crevice between the back cushions. Then, I created an inside back panel with a center welted seam that gives the impression of "cushion lines" (albeit mock ones) that echo the shape of the detached seat cushions below.

Older furniture sometimes has what I call "semi-detached" cushions. Although these cushions cannot be removed, they do have individual definition with welted edges and crevices between them. It's a detail you can play up, or play down, depending on how you fit the cover.

What To Do About "Arm Bumps"?

Some upholstered furniture has "arm bumps" at the back edges of the arms where they intersect with the outside back. Hmm. This bumpy situation calls for some extra fitting. Here are two ways to navigate these bumps during slipcover shell construction.

- Address this fitting issue while fitting, shaping and clipping the inside arm panels around the arm joints (the curved seams where the inside arms are joined to the inside back). Study how the center-back edge of these arm panels drape over the arm bumps. As necessary, pin-fit and mark one or two darts to eliminate this excess fabric. Stitch these darts at the same time you stitch the arm-joint seams.

- Wait to fit the outer back edges of the arm panels until it's time to attach the outside back panel to the assembled shell. At this point, you can create several small pleats or one or two larger tucks to remove the excess fabric and allow the arm panels to fit smoothly into the outside back panel seams. This was my fitting strategy for the floral loveseat's arm bump, as shown below. (These photos also illustrate a laced closure. See Lace Me Up on page 82 for instructions.)

Taking small tucks in the excess fabric is one way to fit the back edge of the inside arm panel over an awkward arm bump.

Fit Different Arm Styles

Arms come in all different shapes and sizes. Here are techniques for fitting several unique arm styles and, in the last example, for fitting a chair with no arms at all!

One-Piece Inside Arm and Arm Front

Sometimes it makes sense to omit a separate arm front panel and instead, cut and fit a single panel to cover both the inside-arm and arm-front areas. This is how I made the arms for this chair's patchwork cover. (I confess that I did not invent this fitting technique. I followed the construction of the underlying upholstery.) This technique can work with square or partially square arms. It does not work, however, with scrolled and sloped arms.

● Instructions

1 To determine the cutting dimensions of this single inside-arm and arm-front panel, measure the distance from the arm joint back edge down the length of the arm and over the arm front to the deck. Add 2" for seam allowances and fitting ease. Also add the tuck-in allowance if your furniture has a T-shaped seat like this chair. The resulting measurement is the panel's *cut width*. To determine the panel's cut length, follow the inside arm measuring and cutting dimensions instructions beginning on page 24 in Chapter 2.

2 Cut two panels in the dimensions determined in step 1.

3 To fit each inside arm panel, place the panel over the arm. Position the panel to allow for adequate seam allowances to join this panel to the inside back, outside arm and outside back panels, as well as the deck. For the latter joining, make sure to allow adequate fabric for the tuck-in (if any) at the lower edge of the arm front. Secure the panel with T-pins.

4 Pin-fit the excess fabric at the arm front vertical edges and mark the stitching lines as shown in the photo at right.

5 Stitch these "darts" as you continue with the inner shell construction.

This muslin mock-up shows the pin-fitting marking of two vertical "darts" along the arm front inner and outer edges. You will stitch just a few inches of dart at the outer edge—just enough to create and secure the arm panel's upper/outer corner shape. Stitch the interior "dart" down the entire length of the pinned panel edges.

Sloping Arm with Rolled Outer Edge and Scroll Front

The arms on this chair present several fitting challenges: they slope; their width gradually increases from the chair's shoulder to the arm front; and they have a scrolled (not square) silhouette which, as a consequence, creates a scrolled (asymmetrical) arm front. Finally, they do not have traditional curving arm joints—their joints run parallel to the inside back.

Yikes! What a roller coaster ride. Before you take a pass on a chair or sofa with similar arm features, remember the essential rule of slipcover fitting: *Follow the underlying upholstery seams and joints.* The fitting solution is not as hard as you might think.

● Instructions

1 To accommodate this arm style, begin by measuring between the vertical arm joints. Add 2" for seam allowances and fitting ease and trim the previously cut inside back panel to this adjusted width.

2 To fit the sloping arms, each inside arm panel must be cut in two sections and joined in a seam that matches the underlying upholstery seam. The seam on this chair is located about three-fourths of the way up the arm slope. Cut generously sized panels to fit these arm sections.

3 To fit and join each pair of inside arm panels, place the panels on the arm and turn back the seam allowances on each section to match the upholstery seam, clipping and notching the section edges to fit each other (just as you would if fitting and joining the inside-back and inside arm-panels in a curved arm joint). Pin and mark the stitching lines of this seam as shown in the photo on the next page. Remove the panels from the chair and stitch the seam.

4 The next step of the inner-shell construction process is to pin-fit and attach the arm-front panels to the inside arm panels. For this arm style, you must first shape the arm-front panels to mirror the shape of the scrolled arms. Place one panel over an arm front and trace the scroll outline. Remove the panel from the chair, add seam allowances around the side and upper edges and trim the panel into the required shape. Use this shaped panel as a pattern to cut the second arm front panel. Baste welting around the panel side and upper edges, as desired.

5 Pin each arm front panel around the extended front edge of its corresponding inside arm panel. Mark the stitching line as shown in the photo at right. *Note: Refer back to step 6 of Construct the Inner Shell on page 59 to join the arm-front and inside-arm panels.*

6 Continue the inner shell construction by stitching the assembled inside-arm panels to the inside back panel edges. Pin-fit the inner upper edges of the inside arm to fit the chair shoulders by creating tucks or darts.

7 Trim the upper edges of the outside-arm panels to mirror the slope of the chair's arms and upholstery. Pin-fit each panel to the inside-arm panel so that the curved seam is under the roll of the upholstered arm. After stitching these panels, the cover should fit smoothly down, over and under the slopes and curves of this arm. Continue with the remaining shell constructions.

Lower Inside Arm Panel

Arm Front Panel

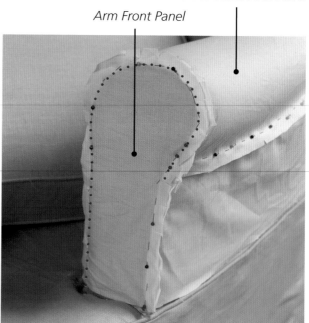

After pin-fitting the scrolled arm front panel to the extended edge of the inside arm panel, mark the stitching line. Note: This muslin sample does not depict the required lower-edge seam and tuck-in allowances.

Lower Inside Arm Panel   Upper Inside Arm Panel

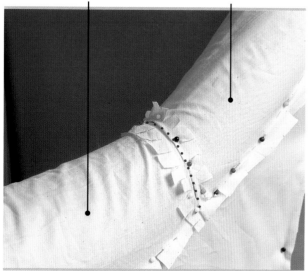

This photo illustrates several arm pinning and fitting techniques. Focus on the clipped edges of the arm panels that traverse across the rounded arm at a slight diagonal. When stitched, this seam will join the upper and lower inside arm panels.

Outside Arm Panel   Assemble Inside Arm Panels

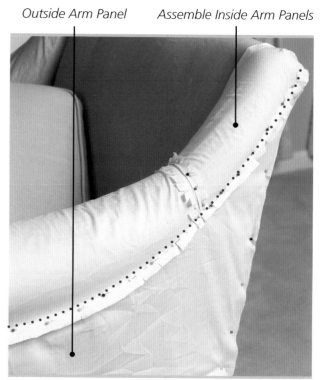

Trim the outside arm panel's upper edge to mirror the slope of the arm, then pin-fit this panel to the inside arm.

Square Arm with Slope

This little boudoir chair with its faded upholstery and nicked wood frame was obviously someone's favorite seat at one time. I knew immediately where its new home should be when I purchased it at an estate sale. I whipped up a new cover in soft cotton chenille, and gave it to my mother. Now, it's her favorite seat après bath. The chair's toss-and-tuck shell had no significant fitting issues, except for the sloping arms of its wood frame.

● Instructions

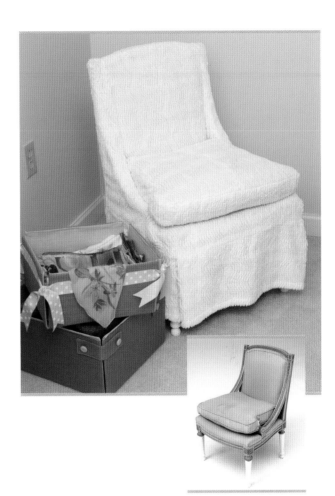

1 The shell construction for this chair begins with the arms, which creates a different order for the remaining shell construction steps. Follow the construction order presented here, and return to the universal construction techniques presented in Chapter 3, when indicated.

2 To cover arms like these, you will cut and assemble three panels: an arm strip that covers the arm's upper-sloping surface and connects to the outer-back panel; one triangular-shaped inner-arm panel; and one triangularl-shaped outer-arm panel. These panels will cover the arm frame's top surface and fill in the open space between the arm frame and the chair seat.

3 To determine the cutting dimensions of the arm strip cut, measure from the interior edge of the arm frame to the chair outside back edge at the widest point. (See number 4 in the photo on the next page for a reference point regarding this measurement.) Add 1" to this measurement. The resulting figure is the strip's *cut width*. Measure the arm length along the frame's top surface, starting at the chair's shoulder, going down the length of the slope and over the front edge of the frame. Add 1" for seam allowances and the tuck-in allowance (as needed). The resulting figure is the strip's *cut length*. Cut two strips in these dimensions.

Soft bathrobe-weight chenille makes an excellent—and washable—slipcover which has transformed this little chair into a comfortable boudoir seat. Note: The pink and green fabric boxes are mini-slipcovered storage units you can make, too. They are featured in my book Decorative Storage. *See Resources on page 143 for ordering information.*

4 Trace the triangular shape of the arm frame sides on muslin, add seam allowances to all edges and, for the inside panel, add the tuck-in allowance at the lower edge. Cut two inside arm and two outside arm panels in these dimensions.

5 Pin-fit the strip's outer edge to the outside arm panel as shown in the first photo on page 95, and trim the excess strip fabric. Form darts to fit the strip to the chair's square shoulders. Remove these panels from the chair and stitch the strip and outside-arm panels together.

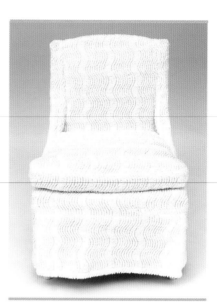

6 Place the partially assembled arm panels on the chair again. Pin-fit each inside arm panel to the inner edge of its strip inner edge as shown in the second photo on page 95. Remove these panels from the chair and stitch the strip and inside arm panels together.

7 Place the assembled arms on the chair again. Refer to number 2 in the second photo on page 95 to attach each inside-arm panel to the lower edges of the inside-back panel.

8 Refer to the inner shell construction techniques on page 62 of Chapter 4 to complete the inner shell by attaching the inside back and inside arm lower edges to the side, back, and edges.

9 Refer to the outer shell construction techniques beginning on page 68 to join the outside back panel to the inside back upper edge and outside arm back edges. *Note:* Stitch completely around the side, upper, and side edges of the outside back panel … there is no zipper insertion seam.

10 Refer to Chapter 5 to assemble and attach your chosen skirt to the slipcover shell. Refer to Chapter 3 to cover any detached seat or back cushions with slipcover fabric.

Arm Strip Inside Back Panel

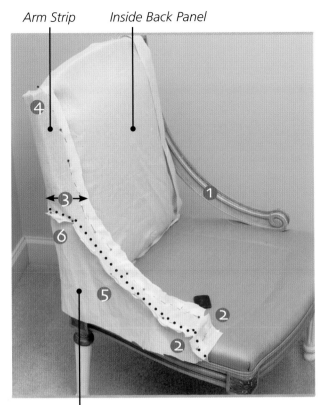

Outside Arm Panel

5 Pin the outside arm panel to the lower portion of the strip's outer edge, and mark the stitching line.

6 At the point where the arm frame connects with the outer back, clip, trim and pin the arm strip and outside arm panel to create a horizontal seam, as shown; mark the stitching line.

Arm Strip Inside Back Panel

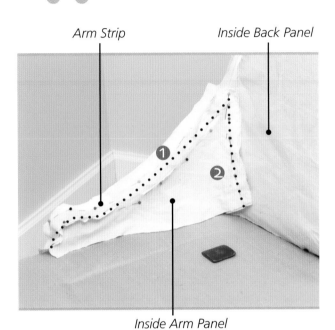

Inside Arm Panel

This muslin mock-up tells the construction story of these arm covers.

1 The uncovered frame in the photo's background reveals the arm's shape, especially the open "triangle" between the frame and the chair seat.

2 The arm strip covers the entire top surface of the arm and its front edge. Clip the strip at the front corners to allow square corners to be sewn when the strip is joined to the outside and inside arm panels.

3 The strip's cut width must be wide enough to span the distance between the arm's inner edge and the chair's outside back edge at its widest point, as indicated by this line.

4 Form darts to fit the strip to the chair's square shoulders.

The fitting story continues inside the chair:

1 Pin the arm strip's inner edge to the inside arm panel's upper edge, and mark the stitching line.

2 Pin the inside arm panel to the inside back panel, and mark the stitching line.

Wing Arms

Think of the wings of a wing-back chair as arm parts. This makes sense if you view the arms as beginning at the chair's shoulders. The points where the arms bend … where they extend forward … are the "elbows." For purposes of the following instructions, consider the seam and joint where these sections are joined as the "elbow joint."

1 Study the underlying upholstery on the chair's inside arms and, in all likelihood, you will find a seam, joint or crevice where the inside arm meets the inside wing. This seam and joint defines the two inside arm sections. Look for a similar seam and joint where the outside arm meets the outside wing. If there are no seams or joints, you're in luck for you can cut single-panel inside and/or outside arms that will have an overall L shape.

2 Assuming these seams or joints exist, follow the instructions given in Chapter 2 for measuring and determining the cutting dimensions of the inside and outside arm panels, excluding the wing portions of these chair sections. Also measure the inside and outside wing sections and cut appropriately sized panel for each.

3 Pin-fit the inside arm panels to the chair, clipping the upper edge seam allowances over the elbow joint just as you would for the traditional arm joint.

The wings of this chair can be viewed as extensions of the arms. To cover them, you will cut, fit and join an upper extension for each inside arm and outside arm panel. Then you will treat these joined panels as one panel as you continue with shell construction.

Inside Wing Panel

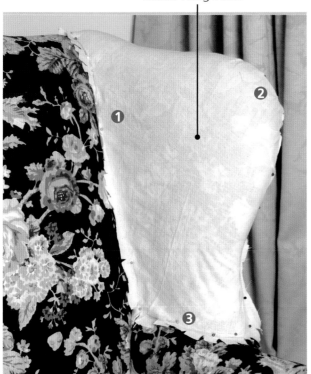

Follow these steps to fit and mark the stitching lines on the inside wing panel.

1 Smooth the inside wing panel into the inside back crevice, and mark the stitching line where it will be joined to the inside back.

2 Form tucks or darts around the outer edge to conform the panel to the shape of the wing.

3 Clip the lower edge to conform with the curve of the elbow joint, and mark the stitching line where it will be joined to the inside arm panel.

4 Pin-fit the inside wing panels to the inside wings, creating darts or tucks around the wing's outer curved edge, fitting the panel's inner edge to conform to the chair's inside back crevice, and clipping the panel's lower edge to fit around the elbow joint, as shown at left.

5 Stitch the inside arms to the inside wings and thereafter treat them as single panels as you continue to construct the inner shell.

6 Repeat this process to pin-fit, trim and assemble the outside arm and outside wing panels, again treating them as single panels as you complete the outer shell construction.

Square Arm and Square Back

This tuxedo-style sofa has straight, squared-edged arms that intersect at right angles with the flat, square-edged back. Curved arm and elbow joints, arm bumps and rounded shoulders are noticeably absent, making this arm construction the easiest of all the featured projects. In fact, the construction technique for covering this arm style is similar to making a box-edge cushion cover. Consult the box-edge cover instructions, beginning on page 00 of Chapter 3 as you review the following instructions.

Arm fitting issues are noticeably absent when the back and arms of the furniture are square and are the same height, a feature of this tuxedo-style sofa.

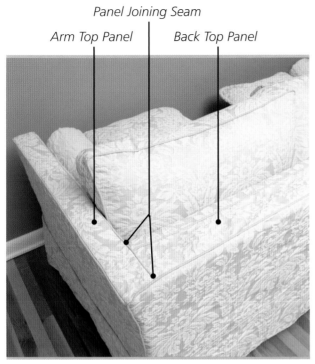

Panel Joining Seam

Arm Top Panel   Back Top Panel

The arm top panel joined to the short end of the back top panel will look like this. The dotted line indicates the panels' joining seam.

1 For this slipcover, you will measure and cut the following panels: inside back, outside back, deck, inside arms, outside arms, and skirt panels. You will also cut two *arm top panels* (that incorporate the arm front panels) and one *back top panel;* see the photos above to identify these additional panels.

2 To determine the cutting dimensions of the arm top panels, measure the arm length front to back; also measure the arm front from its upper front corner to the point where the skirt will be attached. Combine these measurements and add 2". This is the arm top panel's *cut length*. Measure the arm width and add 2". This is the arm top panel's *cut width*. Cut two panels in these dimensions.

3 To determine the cutting dimensions of the back top panel, measure the length of the sofa across its top edge. Multiply the arm width measurement by two, and subtract this figure from the sofa length measurement. Add 2". The resulting figure is the back top panel *cut length*. Measure the depth of the sofa's top back surface and add 2". This is the back top panel's cut width. Cut one panel in these dimensions.

4 Because the sofa's back and top arms are the same height and intersect at right angles, it makes sense to include the back top panel in the arm construction. Begin by basting welting to the long edges of each arm top panel. Also baste welting to the inner edge of the back top panel.

5 Place the back top panel on the sofa top back and align the arm top panels over the arms. Pin-fit and mark the short seams to join the arm top panels to the short ends of the back top panel, referring to the photo at left.

6 Pin-fit, trim and stitch the inside arm panels to the inner edges of the arm top panels; clip the arm top panels at the front corners of the sofa arms to facilitate pivoting at the corners of the inside arm panels. (Again, this process is similar to joining a box-band to the top and bottom panels of a box-band cushion cover.)

7 Proceed with the remaining steps of the inner shell construction.

8 During outer shell construction, repeat the process in step 5 above to join the outside arm panels to the outer edges of the arm top panels. Proceed with the remaining steps of the outer shell construction.

Overall Tub Shape

There's hardly a straight edge on this chair ... the back curves, the arms slope and the interior is concave. A fitting nightmare? you may ask. Not really. Once the inside back takes shape, the remaining construction of this all-in-one cover is relatively easy.

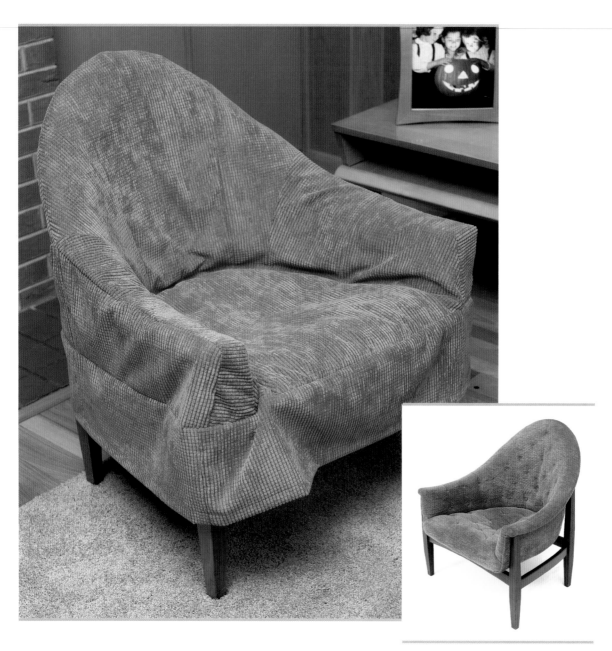

Kelly green chenille changes to a plush persimmon. And shabby Danish modern in transformed into a cozy casual tub chair. A little padding in the deck panel beefs up the chair's sagging seat, too. Aren't slipcovers amazing?

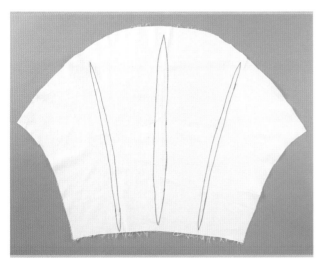

This muslin pattern of the inside back panel includes three contour-style darts, which help shape the panel to the chair's interior curves.

1 For a chair like this one, I recommend that you do not measure and pre-cut rectangular panels for its inner and outer shell. This effort takes more time and uses more fabric than is necessary. Instead, trace the shape of the various chair sections onto muslin, using the upholstery seams as your guide for determining the shape of these panels. Remove the muslin pieces from the chair, add 1" beyond their traced lines and cut out the patterns. Use these patterns to cut panels from your slipcover fabric. *Note:* See the photoson page 102 which identify the panels of this slipcover.

2 The inside back panel presents the most critical fitting issue for a chair of this style. If upholstery seams are absent (as was the case with the featured chair), then fitting this panel requires the creation of three to five narrow vertical darts, similar to the contour darts you would find in a fitted blouse or at the waist of shift-style dress. These darts are illustrated in the muslin pattern shown above.

3 To create a similar pattern, place muslin on the chair's inside back area, molding it into the concave shape and use T-pins to secure the edges. Pin-fit the excess fabric into equally spaced vertical darts and mark the dart stitching lines. Also trim and shape the muslin at its outer edges to conform to the overall curved shape of the inside back. Use this pattern to transfer the dart stitching lines onto the panel cut from your slipcover fabric. Stitch these darts before beginning the inner shell construction.

4 To add some extra "cush" to your chair's seat, try padding the deck. Cut two deck panels from the slipcover fabric. Baste these panels, wrong-sides together, leaving approximately 6" unstitched. Insert polyester fiberfill into the deck interior to plump it up, then baste the opening closed. Thereafter, treat the double layered deck panel as one layer.

5 Refer to Assembly Overview on page 102 for a summary of this slipcover's construction.

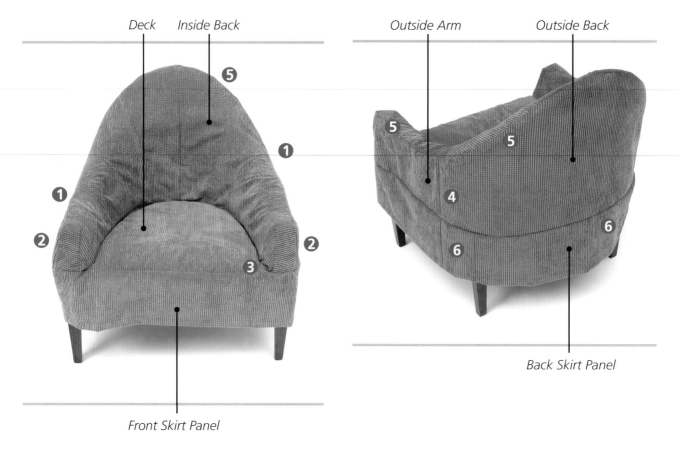

Deck   Inside Back

Outside Arm   Outside Back

Front Skirt Panel

Back Skirt Panel

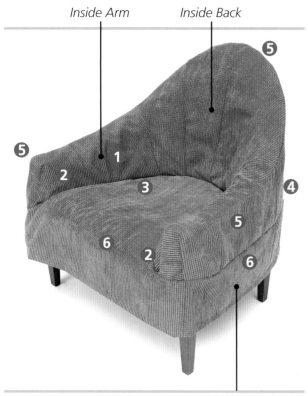

Inside Arm   Inside Back

Side Skirt Panel

Assembly Overview

Viewed from various angles, this slipcover reveals its simple construction.

1. The shaped/darted inside back is joined to the inside arms.
2. The inside arms are fitted/shaped with vertical darts at their front edges.
3. The padded deck is joined to the lower edges of the inner shell.
4. The outside arm panels are joined to the side edges of the outside back panel.
5. The inner and outer shell sections are joined in one long curved seam that begins at the arm front lower edge, pivots at the arm front upper edge corner, continues up, around and down the edge, and ends at the opposite arm's lower edge.
6. The skirt is assembled and attached to the shell's lower edge. Note: The skirt panels have been cut/pieced so their joining seams align with the shell seams.

Work Around An Exposed Frame

This slipcover's construction combines a number of fitting techniques, such as tucks to shape the curved shoulders along the upper back edge and darts to shape the deck's front corners. Been there, done that, of course. The new techniques with this project are the cutouts, edge finishing and double back closures needed to fit the cover around and over the chair's wood arms, and my "secret" solution for molding fabric over slightly mounded or concave surfaces. Whew! There's a lot of fitting and fabric preparation going on here … but the end result is worth the effort. This chair is a real charmer!

This slipcover project illustrates a number of fitting technique to work around the exposed wood arms of this Queen Anne style chair.

1 This chair's deck (seat) is broad and slightly mounded in the center, and its inside back is slightly concave. Although these are nice features on an upholstered chair, they create a slipcover dilemma: How to fit flat panels of fabric over these less-than-flat surfaces? My solution is to add low-loft cotton quilt batting as an inner layer and use muslin or broadcloth as the lining. This results in a quilt "sandwich" of sorts for the deck, inside back and outside back panels. The batting provides just enough extra fabric "mass" to help mold it over these contoured surfaces. In the following steps as you cut each of these panels, also cut a companion layer of low-loft batting and your chosen lining material; sandwich the batting between the face and lining panels and baste their edges. Treat the three layers as a single layer during the ensuing fitting and assembly steps.

2 Cutting panels for this chair's slipcover, like the tub chair project on page 100, is best accomplished by setting aside the traditional measuring of chair sections. Instead, begin by placing the whole cloth over the inside back of the chair; if using a large print like the featured one, adjust the fabric until you're satisfied with the position of prominent motifs. *Remember:* This panel is your chair's focal point; how you position the print here will influence all other cut panels. Cut an inside back panel 3" wider and longer than the chair's inside back. The extra width will be used to create self-facings around the arm joints; the extra length will be used at the lower edge for a small tuck-in into the deck and inside back crevice.

Inside Back Panel   *Inner and Outer Shell Assembly Seam*

Extended Front Skirt Panel   *Deck Panel*   *Skirt Side Panel*

Outside Back Panel   *Inner and Outer Shell Assembly Seam*

Skirt Back Panel

3 Repeat the step 2 process to position the fabric on the deck, lining up and matching the print pattern vertically and horizontally to correspond with the pattern placement on the inside back panel. Cut the deck panel at least 3" to 4" wider and longer than the actual deck size.

4 Repeat the step 2 and step 3 processes to cut the outside back panel, taking care to position and match the print pattern to the inside back at its upper edge. Cut this panel 3" wider than the chair's outside back width.

5 Use darts or tucks to shape the inside back panel at the chair's shoulders, and use darts, as well, to fit the deck panel to the front corners of the chair's seat/deck. Stitch the lower edge of the inside back panel to the back edge of the deck panel. Place these assembled panels on the chair, right-side down.

6 The curve where the wood arms intersect with the chair back and chair seat are the "arm joints." Carefully clip the side edges of the inside back panel and the deck panel to ease the fabric around these arm joints—just as you would if clipping and fitting the arm joint seams of a full slipcover. Mark the stitching line. Use the photo on page 58 in Chapter 4 as a reference.

7 Remove the shell from the chair. Press under the clipped seams at each joint and topstitch these edges to finish them.

8 To assemble the inner and outer shell, pin, and then stitch the inside and outside back panels in the seam identified in the photos at left. Press under the seam allowances of the remaining open edges to create self-facings; topstitch these edges to finish them.

Press under the seam allowance that has been fitted around each arm joint and topstitch to finish this edge.

The separate skirt panels and shell's open edges allow a peek-a-boo glimpse of the chair's underlying upholstery. It's a quaint, shabby chic look that I've seen in many high-end decorating magazines.

9 This slipcover features a scalloped skirt, consisting of four separate panels: a front panel that extends around the front corners of the deck to butt the front edges of the arm frame; two side panels that butt the back edges of the arm frame and continue to the outside back; and one back panel that spans the outside back width of the chair. These panels are identified in the photos on page 104. *Note:* The featured skirt is attached approximately 1" below the deck's upper edge and has a finished length of 6".

10 To create this skirt style, each panel must have finished side edges. Thus, you must cut each skirt panel 1" longer than the area it will span. Follow the instructions given on page 75 in Chapter 5 to trace the scallop pattern on each panel's lower edge. Instead of creating facings for of just the scallops, cut full linings for each skirt panel from muslin or broadcloth. Pin the skirt and lining panels, right-sides together, and stitch the scallops across each panel's lower edge, but also stitch the panel side edges in ½" seams. When you turn these panels right-side out, their side edges will be finished.

11 Pin, then stitch each skirt panel to the lower edge of its corresponding shell section.

12 Place the completed shell on the chair, and mark the desired location of the ribbon ties along the open back edges. Place each ribbon end underneath the shell's topstitched edge at its marked position and machine tack it in place, stitching over the previous topstitches. *Note:* I used four pairs of 12"-long ribbon ties at each open edge; you may decide to cut longer ribbon lengths and/or use fewer ties.

Chapter 7

Done-in-a-Day Covers

After making a hem-to-haw slipcover, you might want to take a break (you've earned it!).
The slipcover concepts in this chapter are quick and easy …
and can be completed in about a day.

*Chairs made with woven vinyl have seats and backs that stick to arms and legs in
warm weather. Solution? A one-piece cushion or cover that's secured to the chair's
back with an "envelope" panel and attached to the seat frame with fabric ties. This
cover concept works on other chairs that have small frames and seats and backs that
are the same width, such as folding aluminum lawn chairs and card table chairs.*

No More Sticky Vinyl

Summer—hot. Vinyl—sticky. Cover the seat/back of a porch/patio chair with a cool and comfortable cushion made from an indoor/outdoor stripe fabric.

Materials

Indoor-outdoor fabric in determined yardage

Coordinating purchased piping in determined yardage

Low-loft quilt batting

Instructions

1 Drape a tape measure down the inside back and forward over the seat of the chair as shown. Add 1" to this measurement; this is the panel *cut length*. Measure the back and seat width and add 1"; this is the panel *cut width*.

2 To determine the required fabric yardage, draw a sample layout that includes two panels in the previously determined dimensions. Also, draw an envelope panel that is 1" wider than the panel's cut width and is between 8" and 12" long. *Note:* The envelope panel's extra width is to accommodate the depth of your chair's frame. Increase its width if the frame is deeper than 1". Cut a longer or shorter envelope panel depending on how much fabric you want to see on the chair's outside back.

Measure the chair's interior width and length as shown; add 1" seam allowances to each measurement to determine the panel's cutting dimensions.

3 To determine the required piping yardage, measure the cushion panel's perimeter and add 2" to 3".

4 Cut two cushion panels and one envelope panel from the fabric. Use the cushion panel as a pattern to cut one batting panel. Also cut two 1½" x 18" fabric strips for ties.

5 Baste the batting panel to the wrong side of one cushion panel, and thereafter treat them as a single layer. Baste the piping around the edges of this panel.

6 Place the piped cushion panel, right-side up, on the chair, and fold it to conform to the angle of the seat and back juncture. Mark the tie placements at the folded edges of this panel.

7 To make each pair of ties, press under ½" on all edges of the strip. Fold the strip in half widthwise, wrong-sides together. Topstitch close to the strip's folded edge. Cut the strip into two equal lengths.

8 Baste the overlapped cut ends of two ties and at one marked location on the cushion panel; position tie's ends within the panel's seam allowance. Repeat to baste the second pair of ties to the opposite marked edge of this panel.

9 Press under and topstitch a double ½" hem on the lower edge of the envelope panel. Pin this panel, wrong-side down, over the right side upper edge of the unbatted cushion panel. Baste these panels together.

10 Pin and then stitch the cushion panels together, making sure not to catch the ties in the seams and leaving about 10" to 12" unstitched on one edge for turning. Turn the cushion layers right-side out through the opening. Turn under the seam allowances on the open edge and whipstitch the opening closed.

11 Slide the cushion envelope over the chair back upper edge. Tie the ties around the chair frame at the seat back.

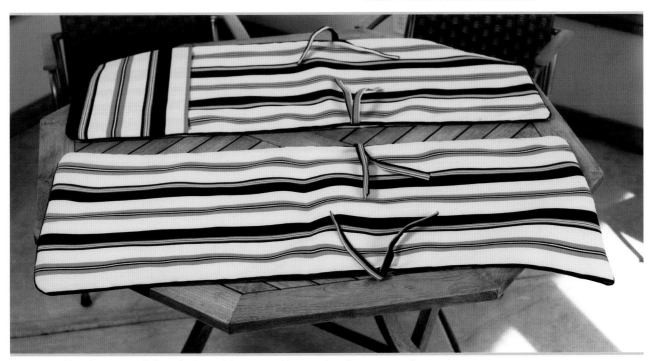

Front and back views of this chair cushion reveal its so-simple construction.

Made-for-the-Shade

The same striped fabric used on the porch chairs takes a spin on this octagonal teak dining table. Pie-wedge panels cut on the cross grain are edged in scalloped flaps to replicate a classic striped umbrella.

This cover concept works on a square, round, or multi-sided table that is symmetrical, such as the featured octagonal table. The construction is easy: Cut four wedge-shaped sections, on the straight grain or cross grain of a striped fabric, and join them in crisscrossing seams. Add a flapped-panel skirt—mirrors the table's shape.

Align the muslin quarter-panel inner edges with the masking tape edges, as shown. Use tailor's chalk to trace the table edge on the muslin.

The stripes on your table cover can flow one of two ways: either straight grain (above) or cross grain (below). You decide... just make sure to cut four identical panels.

Materials

54"-wide indoor-outdoor striped fabric in determined yardage. *Note:* 3 yd. of fabric were required to cover the featured 42"-diameter table.

Muslin to make a quarter-section panel

Coordinating purchased piping in determined yardage (optional)

1"-wide masking tape

Instructions

1 Measure the diameter of your table and add 2". On graph paper, draw a square in these dimensions, and then divide this square into four equal sections. Cut a square from muslin in the resulting quarter-square dimensions.

2 Divide the table top surface into four equal sections using crisscrossing lengths of masking tape.

3 Place the muslin quarter-panel on the table with two of its cut edges aligned with the tape edges. Use tailor's chalk to trace the table's outer edge on the muslin, as shown in the opposite photo.

4 Remove the muslin panel from the table and mark cutting lines ½" beyond the traced table edge. Cut the muslin on the marked cutting lines.

5 Use this muslin pattern to cut four identical panels from the striped fabric. Position the pattern on the straight grain (like the featured table cover) or on the cross grain, as desired, as shown in the middle and bottom photos at left.

6 Pair two panels and pin their diagonal edges, making sure that the stripes are exactly matched; stitch the pinned seam. Repeat to pin and stitch the remaining two panels. Press all seams open. Again, with stripes matching, pin and then stitch the joined panels in a seam that crisscrosses the previous joining seams. Press this seam open, too.

7 To cut the skirt panels, measure one table edge and add 1"; this is the panel's *cut width*. Add 1" to the desired finished length of each panel; this is the panel-cut length. The featured skirt panels have a finished length of 6". Cut two panels per table edge in these determined dimensions. *Note:* For a round table, measure the table top circumference. Divide this measurement by the desired number of skirt panels and add 1". The resulting figure is the panel's *cut width*.

8 To determine the required piping yardage to edge the skirt panels, measure one panel's side and lower edges and multiply this measurement by the total number of skirt panels.

9 If desired, curve the lower corners of each pair of skirt panels by tracing around a round object, such as a glass or measuring cup. Trim the excess fabric beyond the curved lines.

10 To assemble each skirt panel, baste piping around the side and lower edges of one panel. Stitch a second panel to the piped panel around the same edges. Turn the panels right-side out and press the stitched edges flat. Baste the panel upper edges.

11 To finish the cover, stitch the skirt panels around the edge of the assembled top panel. Press the skirt panel seam allowances toward the top panel. Topstitch around the top panel, ¼" from its edge, to secure these seam allowances.

For this table cover, 6"-long skirt flaps seem just right. You may choose to make your flaps longer.

Grill Cover-Up

When the outdoor grilling season is over, you can store your grill in style with this easy to make cover-up. Start with a circle of fabric, cut and finish an opening for the handle of the grill lid, and create a drawstring closure with grommets and decorative cording.

The mitered stripe construction technique used in the Made-for-the-Shade table cover on page 110 is repeated on this fitted cover for a small kettle grill.

Materials

Note: Materials are given to make a cover-up that fits a 24" x 36" grill with domed lid (measurements are approximate).

1½ yd. of 54"-wide indoor/outdoor fabric. *Note:* A pieced cover-up made from a stripe fabric, like the featured project, requires 3 yd. of fabric.

32 grommets and grommet setting tools

5 yd. of narrow cording for cover tie

Instructions

1 Cut a 50"-diameter circle from the fabric. Or, if desired, refer to the Made-in-the-Shade table cover instructions on page 110 to cut and join four wedge sections in the desired mitered stripe pattern to create a pieced circle.

2 The lid handle opening on the featured project measures 6" x 1¼", and its construction is similar to that of a bound buttonhole. To make this opening, measure the lid handle width and the distance between the braces that secure it to the lid (adding extra inches, as necessary, to accommodate the actual handle length). Note these measurements.

3 Fold the cut (or pieced) circle into quarters and mark its center. Measure and draw a handle opening, centered side-to-side and upper edge-to-lower edge, relative to this mark, using the measurements determined in step 2.

4 From scrap fabric, cut a facing panel that is 3" longer and 3" wider than the marked opening. On the wrong side of this facing, measure and draw the opening in the dimensions determined in step 2. Make sure to draw the opening centered side-to-side and upper edge-to-lower edge. Press under ½" on the facing edges and topstitch them.

5 Pin the facing to the fabric circle, right-sides together, matching the marked lines. Stitch the facing to the circle on the marked lines. Slit the layers down the center of the opening and diagonally to the corners as shown below.

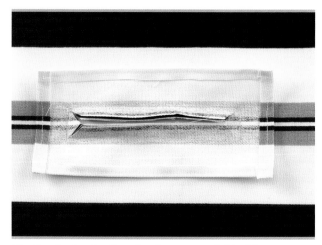

Pin the facing to the circular cover, right-sides together and with stitching lines aligned. Stitch on the marked lines. Slit the interior section of the facing cover as shown.

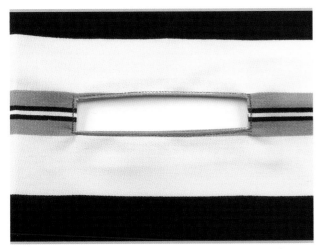

After turning the facing to the cover's wrong side, edgestitch around the handle opening.

Install equally spaced grommets around the edge of the cover-up. Thread the cording through the grommet holes.

6 Turn the facing to the cover's wrong side through the slit opening. Press the edges flat. On the right side, edgestitch around the opening.

7 Press under ½" twice on the cover edge and topstitch the hem. Or, if desired, finish the circle edge with purchased piping or cording and a self facing; see the Welted Hem instructions on page 72.

8 Measure and mark an even number of equally spaced grommet positions around the edge of the circle. Install the grommets at the marked positions. Thread the cording through the grommet holes. Tie the cording ends in overhand knots.

9 Place the cover over the grill with the lid handle inserted through the opening. Pull the cording at the cover's lower edge to gather the excess fabric around the base of the grill and tie the cording ends.

Dining Two Ways

Switch the chairs, add different chairs slipcovers and a fitted tablecloth, and it's a whole new dining experience.

Over the years we've acquired two sets of vintage dining chairs. The '50s mahogany chairs look very traditional (inset photo), but the '70s-era metal and cane chairs have a more contemporary feel. I switch one set for another at holidays and celebrations and sometimes use the seat and back slipcovers I've sewn for each set. My dining room never looks the same twice!

Chair Back Cover

● Materials

Armless dining chair with a square or rectangular back

1 yd. of 54"-wide fabric.
Note: This yardage is enough to make two covers for armless dining chairs with square backs up to 16" high. For chairs with taller backs, add ¼ yd. per 3" of additional height.

A little slipcover makes a large dining statement. This style works best with dining chairs that have square-edged backs.

● Instructions

1 Measure the width, height and depth of your chair's back.

2 To make a back cover for a chair with a uniform depth, cut one cover panel in these dimensions:
width + (*depth* ÷ 2) + 1" x (*height* x 2) + 2"
Example: For a chair back measuring 20" x 22" x 2", you would cut a cover panel in these dimensions:
20" + (2" ÷ 2) + 1" x (22" x 2) + 2", or 22" x 46".

3 Finish the cover's lower edges by pressing under and topstitching ½" doubled hems on the panel's short edges.

4 Assembling this cover is much like making a pillowcase. Fold the panel in half lengthwise and align the finished edges. Pin, then stitch the remaining raw edges together. Turn the cover right-side out and slide it over the back of your chair.

5 To make a cover for a chair back with a graduated depth, like the featured chair, measure the width and height of your chair's back. For the depth, measure the chair's depth where it is the shallowest. Use these dimensions and the formula given in step 2 on page 117 to cut one cover panel.

6 To cut the side inset panel, place your fabric on the floor, wrong-side up. Place the chair on its side over the fabric and trace the shape of its edge on the fabric. Add ½" seam allowances to the side and upper edges, and add 1" to the lower edge. Cut out this panel and use it as a pattern for the second inset panel.

7 Finish the lower edges of the primary and side panels with doubled ½" topstitched hems.

8 Fold the primary panel in half, lengthwise and right-sides together. Pin a side panel between the primary panel raw edges, making sure their hemmed edges are aligned. Stitch the side panels to the primary panel.

9 Turn the cover right-side out and place it over the chair back.

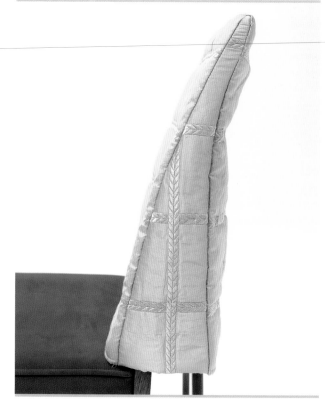

To accommodate a back with a graduated depth, insert a side panel like the one shown here.

Chair Seat Cover

● Materials

Dining chair with upholstered seat and open frame

1 yd. of 54"-wide fabric (enough to make the featured 30" x 30" cover with bias banded edges)

1 yd. each of lining fabric and muslin

Low-loft cotton quilt batting

Fusible-web seam tape

2 large garment snaps

This master/mistress dining chair wears a seat cover made from silk taffeta, which isn't your typical slipcover fabric. However, an inner layer of batting, muslin and lining keep this slippery fabric from sliding around on the seat's surface, and give the seat cover some needed heft.

● Instructions

1 Measure the width and depth of the chair's upholstered seat at its widest and deepest points. Add 2" to each measurement and cut one panel each from the cover fabric, the lining, the batting and the muslin.

2 To replicate the 1"-wide hem band and arm ties, determine the required band length by measuring the seat circumference at the lower edge of its upholstery; add 1 yd. to this measurement. Cut 3"-wide strips of the cover fabric (cut on the bias or straight grain, as desired) and piece the strips, as necessary, to achieve the determined band length. Set the assembled band aside.

3 To fit the seat panel, first create a muslin pattern. Center the muslin on the chair. Fold the excess muslin at the seat's front corners to create vertical darts. Pin and mark the dart stitching lines. *Note:* Refer to the deck fitting instructions in Chapter 4 on page 61 to create these darts.

4 Fold and clip the excess muslin to fit around the arms curves and the back braces, and trace their outlines. This fitting is similar to fitting the arm joints of a full slipcover.

5 Remove the muslin panel from the chair, add ½" seam allowances beyond the traced lines and cut out the pattern.

6 Use this pattern to cut the cover, lining and batting panels. Transfer the dart stitching lines to the wrong side of the cover and lining panels, and to one side of the batting panel.

7 Baste the batting panel to the wrong side of the lining panel matching the dart stitching lines. Thereafter treat the two layers as one layer.

8 Stitch the front corner darts on the cover and lining panels. Trim the excess dart fabric.

9 To assemble the cover and finish its lower edge with a fabric band, pin the cover and lining panels, right-sides together, at the arm and back brace curves only. Stitch these seams, clip/notch the curves, and turn the panels right-side out. Press the seams flat.

10 Baste the remaining cover and lining panel raw edges, wrong-sides together.

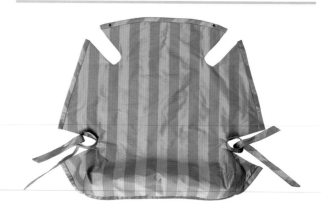

One photo speaks volumes! This overhead view of the featured seat cover illustrates the interior curves that accommodate the chair's arms and back braces.

11 Refer to the Accent Band Hem instructions in Chapter 5 beginning on page 73 to apply a bias-cut hem band with these modifications: The arm and back brace openings create four separate sections that each require a band. For each section, fold under ½" on each band section short edges and align the folds with the cover raw edges before stitching the band.

12 To make the arm ties, cut the remaining hem band strip into two equal lengths. Press under ½" on each strip's short ends. Press under the seam allowances on each strip's long edges. Fold each strip in half widthwise and wrong-sides together, and press the fold. Edgestitch each strip's folded edges.

13 Hand tack a tie around each arm curve.

14 To secure the cover's overlapped edges at the chair's back braces, mark snap locations and hand stitch the snap sections to the cover.

15 Place the cover on the chair. Tie the strips around the arms, overlap the back edges, and snap them together.

Fitted Table Covers

Fitted table covers qualify as slipcovers, and they are incredibly easy to make. The following instructions apply to the full-length table covers. These can go a long way in transforming other less-than-pristine tables into truly functional pieces.

If you can make a box-edge cushion, you can make a fitted table cover...
with pleats and a skirt that brushes the floor.

Materials

Oval, rectangular or shaped table with a serving, library, or dining height

54"-wide fabric in determined yardage

Pre-made welting in yardage to fit around the cover's upper edge (optional)

Instructions

1 *To determine the yardage for a fitted table cover,* measure the width and length of the table top at its widest and longest points; add 1" to each measurement. These are the cutting dimensions of the top panel.

2 Measure the table top perimeter. Refer to the Skirt Panel Cutting Dimensions on page 139 in the Appendix to add seam and pleat or gathering allowances to the perimeter measurement and to determine the overall skirt panel cut width. The skirt panel cut length for all table covers equals the determined finished length + 4½". Also consult the instructions on page 69 in Chapter 5 to plan the panel widths so that the joining seams are concealed within pleats or are positioned at corners where they are less noticeable.

3 Use the top panel and skirt panel cutting dimensions to draw a layout and determine the required yardage to make the cover. If making welting or using purchased trim in the top panel and skirt joining seam, add 4" to the table top perimeter for the required welting or trim yardage.

4 *To make a full-length table cover,* cut the top panel in the determined cutting dimensions and center it, right-side down, over the table top. Trace the shape of the table's top surface on the panel. Remove the panel from the table and draw a cutting line ½" beyond the traced line. Cut this panel on the outer marked line.

5 If desired, baste welting around the edge of the top panel.

6 Piece the skirt panels, short end-to-short end. On the skirt lower edge, press under 2" twice and topstitch the hem.

7 Form the desired number of pleats at the determined intervals around the skirt's upper edge. Baste across the pleat upper edges.

8 Pin the skirt upper edge to the top panel edge with pleats positioned correctly. Stitch the skirt to the top panel. Turn the cover right-side out and place it over the table.

9 *To make a box-edge cover for a rectangular table,* refer to steps 1 and 2 to cut the top panel and skirt panels in the determined dimensions.

10 Assemble the skirt panels, short edge-to-short edge. Press under 2" twice and topstitch the hem on the skirt's lower edge.

11 Refer to the step 9 instructions in Construct a Box-Edge Cushion Cover on page 48 to stitch the skirt panel upper edge to the top panel edges.

12 Turn the cover right-side out and place it over the table.

A full-length fitted table skirt not only looks elegant, it provides hidden storage underneath. This is where my mother keeps her tool box and emergency radio. The storage benefits of home décor fabrications are the focus of projects in Decorative Storage, my first sewing book. See Resources on page 143 for information about this book.

You can make a cover for any table, regardless of its shape, by tracing the outline of its top. I added a little extra drama to this buffet table's upper edge with glued-on decorative braid.

Better Head (and Comfy Feet)

The underlying metal frame may look like a hospital bed, but when I saw it at a consignment store, I knew it had potential. Covered in a masculine brown pinstripe, this bed makes quite a statement in my son's bachelor pad. You can replicate this look on a straight- or curved-edge headboard (and footboard) by making a tight-fitting quilted slipcover.

Instructions are given for the featured full-size headboard and footboard which is covered in 54"-wide fabric, cut on the straight grain. To make a similar cover for a larger headboard, choose a fabric that can be railroaded to avoid piecing panels.

Get the luxe look of expensive upholstered headboards and footboards by covering an old wreck of a bed frame with snug-fitting tailored covers.

● Materials

Twin or full size headboard (and optional footboard)

54"-wide fabric in determined yardage. *Note:* The featured full-size headboard/footboard projects required 6 yd. of fabric.

Cotton lining fabric in determined yardage

High-loft quilt batting

Self-adhesive Velcro hook tape; sew-in Velcro loop tape

● Instructions

The featured headboards and footboards have inner rails spanning their widths to hold the mattress/box springs, as well as brackets to hold the side rails. These structural elements were impediments to making the inner and outer cover panels the same length. Thus, the inner panels stop at the horizontal rail, while the outer panels end at the top of the frame's wheels. If your head/footboard has similar impediments…and you want their outer panels to be longer than their inner panels…just measure and cut appropriately sized panels for each side of the bed frame (head, foot or both).

1 Take the following measurements of your bed frame: head and footboard width, depth and desired (or maximum) finished length of the inner and outer panels. Also measure the head and footboard side and upper-side edges, beginning and ending at the determined finished length of the outer panel. Use these measurements to cut the following panels:

Outer Panel:
   width + 1" x *outer panel finished length* + 2½"
Inner Panel:
   width + 1" x inner panel finished length + 2½"
Band:
   Depth + 1" x *Side* + *Upper* + *Side* + 4"

2 For a curved headboard cover, like the featured project, you must shape the inner and outer panel upper edges. To do this, center one panel side-to-side over the headboard; tape the panel to the board with the panel upper edge extending ½" beyond the board's upper edge. Trace the curved outline of the headboard on the panel. Remove the panel from the headboard and mark a ½" seam allowance beyond the traced line. Trim the excess fabric on this line.

3 Use this shaped panel as a pattern to shape the inner panel and cut one lining and one batting panel for each.

4 Layer the outer panel, batting and lining panel (with fabrics wrong-sides together) and baste their edges. Thereafter treat the three layers as a single layer.

5 Mark the desired stitching lines for machine quilting on the outer panel right side. Stitch these lines.

6 Press under 1" twice on the inner and outer panel lower edges and the band panel short ends, and topstitch their hems.

7 Stitch the band long edges to the inner and outer panels. For a head and footboard with square corners, this assembly is similar to joining a box band panel to a cushion panel; (see Construct a Box-Edge Cushion Cover, pages 45–48).

8 Place the covers over the headboard and footboard. To secure the band lower edge to the bed frame, adhere Velcro hook tape to the frame leg. Mark the corresponding placements of Velcro loop tape on the bands.

9 Remove the cover. Edgestitch a length of Velcro loop tape on the wrong side of the band at each marked location. If the inner panel is shorter than the outer panel, the band will have exposed raw edges. Press under the ½" seam allowance on these raw edges and topstitch them in place.

10 Slide the cover over the head and footboard and adhere the Velcro strips.

A little Velcro helps secure the footboard band panel to the leg of the frame.

Dog House Re-do

When she hears "Bedtime for Belle," our little dog heads straight to her dog crate—and for good reason! I recently rehabbed Belle's bedtime abode with a custom cover that blends right in with the family room décor. Dave says it's over-the-top, but what the heck…Belle's family. You, too, can remodel your precious pooch's home. Follow my paw prints to create a cover that offers lots of curb appeal with decorative trim and multiple closure options for the front door flap.

Materials

54"-wide medium-weight fabric in determined yardage

Decorative trim or cording in determined yardage (optional)

5 coordinating buttons

Narrow cord, such as drapery shade cord

Long needle with large eye (i.e. upholstery needle)

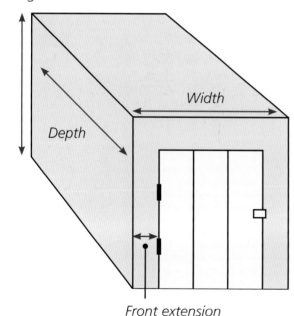

Height

Width

Depth

Front extension

Instructions

1 Refer to the drawing below to measure the width, depth and height of your dog crate. Also measure the width of the crate's front panel from the edges of the door to the front corners. Record these measurements in the chart below.

Crate Dimensions:

width	_____ "
depth	_____ "
height	_____ "
front extension (if any)	_____ "

2 Determine the panel cutting dimensions for the cover using the chart on page 129 and the crate dimensions noted in step 1.

3 Create a sample layout of the cover panels. Refer to the assembly guide below as you create this layout if you are using a print that requires matching.

4 If using decorative trim or welting around the top panel edges, refer to Construct a Box-Edge Cushion on page 47 to baste trim or cording around the edges of the top panel and join the cording ends (as applicable).

5 Finish the front vertical edges of the side panels by pressing under ½" twice and topstitching the hems. Refer to the Construct a Box-Edge Cushion instructions on page 47 to assemble the side, back, and side panels and join them to the top panel.

Panel Cutting Chart

(use the crate dimensions noted above)

1 Top Panel (cut one)   *width* + 1" x   *depth* + 1" = _____" x _____"

2 Left Side Panel   *depth* + *front extension* + 1½" x *height* + 2½" = _____" x _____"

3 Right Side Panel   *depth* + *front extension* + 1½" x *height* + 2½" = _____" x _____"

4 Back Panel   *width* + 1" x *height* + 2½" = _____" x _____"

5 Front Panel   *width* + 1" x *height* + 1" = _____" x _____"

6 Front Panel Lining   *width* + 1" x *height* + 1" = _____" x _____"

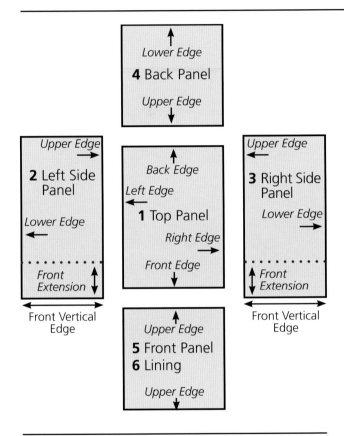

Mark the two rows of button loops with five loops in each row as shown on the front face panel.

6 To make the front panel and door flap, stitch the face and lining panels, right-sides together, around the panel side and lower edges. Trim the seams and corners, and turn the panel right-side out; press the seams flat. Baste the upper raw edges.

7 Measure and mark the button loop placements on the front panel. *Note:* The featured cover has two row of button loops with six loops per row. The first row is positioned across the panel's midpoint. The second row is centered between the midpoint row and the panel's lower edge.

8 Thread the upholstery needle with a length of shade cord. Insert the needle from the lining side through the mark on the face panel and down through the panel to the lining side, taking a ½" stitch. Create a cord loop on the face panel that's large enough to accommodate your chosen buttons. Knot the cord ends on the panel lining side and trim the excess cord. Secure the knot with a dot of fabric glue. Repeat to sew a cord loop at each marked location (for a total of 10 loops). See photos on page 130.

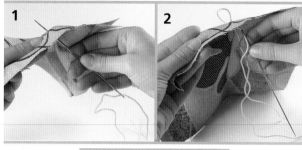

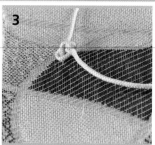

11 Press under 1 " twice on the side and back panel lower edges and topstitch the hem.

12 Place the cover over the crate. Button or roll up the front panel door flap as desired.

1 Insert the threaded needle through the mark from the facing side of the panel and take a ½" stitch.

2 Create a cord loop on the panel face side that's large enough to accommodate the button.

3 Knot the cord ends of the panel lining side and secure with a dot of fabric glue.

9 Stitch the front panel upper edge to the top panel front edge, overlapping the side panels that extend around the top panel front corners (if applicable). Clean finish the raw edges.

10 Sew the five buttons across the front panel upper edge to align with the previously sewn loops.

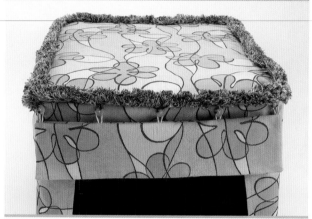

Sew the buttons across the front panel/door flap upper edge to align with the two rows of cord loops.

Consult your pet for his/her door closure preference… in one or two pleats or as a simple fabric roll.

Double Dishin'

Peruse the aisles of the big box stores and you'll find all kinds of casual furniture, including fun chairs that fold up or collapse, and even some with detachable fabric covers, such as the classic butterfly chair. These chairs make great additions to rooms with a casual décor—your child's playroom, a teen's bedroom, even a dorm room or college apartment.

A basic black folding chair finds its groove with a new fabric cover made from a '50s-looking fabric.

For chairs with detachable covers, the re-do is easy—just trace the outline of the slip-on cover and copy it. But, what do you do when the cushion (and its covering fabric) are permanently attached to the chair's frame?

I pondered this very question when I found the featured "dish" chair at my local Target store. I decided that if I couldn't remove and recover the entire seat cushion, I'd do the next best thing: use coordinating fabrics to make a slipcover "cap" to redress the cushion's interior—and fabricate a bonus: a reversible cover!

Materials

Air-Mesh Dish Chair (34½" x 31⅛" x 29½")
available at Target; or other "dish-style"
chair with single cushion attached to a metal
frame

2 yds. each of two 54"-wide coordinating
fabrics

High-loft quilt batting

4 yds. of narrow decorative cording

1½ yds. each of purchased piping and extra-
wide double-fold bias tape

Instructions

1 In designing this cover, I studied the
construction of my chair's cushion and copied
it. The chair's original cushion consists of two
sections: a small U-shaped seat panel and
a large moon-shaped outer panel. When
joined together, these panels create the
shallow "dish" for the seat. I added an outer
band (sized to span the cushion edge that
extends beyond the chair frame). I stitched a
drawstring channel on the band's folded edge
to create the "closure" that secures this cover
over the existing cushion. Keep in the mind
these construction details as your review the
following general instructions.

2 Study the construction of your chair's cushion,
noting seamed panels. Place one fabric, right-
side down, over the cushion and trace the
outline of each panel. Add seam allowances
to the traced edges and cut out the panels.
Use these panels as patterns to cut identical
panels from the second fabric and the batting.

3 Sandwich a batting panel between each fabric
panel (right-side out) and baste their edges.
Thereafter, treat these assembled panels as
one layer.

4 Baste the purchased piping around the inner
edge of the seat panel (on one side—you
choose!).

5 Stitch the seat panel inner edge to the outer
panel lower edge (with fabric matching).
Encase the raw edges of this seam on the
opposite side in double-fold bias tape.

6 Measure the depth of the cushion that
extends beyond the chair frame. Double this
measurement and add 1". The resulting figure
is the cut width of the outer band. Measure the
perimeter of the existing cushion and add 1".

7 Choose one fabric for the band. From the
remaining yardage of this fabric, cut band
strips in the cut width and piece them end-
to-end to create the band assembled length,
as determined in step 6. The resulting piece is
the outer band assembled length.

8 Refer to the Accent Band instructions in
Chapter 6, beginning on page 73, to attach
this band to the outer edge of the cover.

9 To create the drawstring channel, topstitch around the band, ⅝" from its folded edge. At one joining seam, bartack across the seam close to the band fold and close to the seam that joins the band to the cover as shown in the figure at right. Use a seam ripper to carefully open the joining seam between the bar tacks on one side of the band.

10 Use a bodkin or safety pin to thread the decorative cording through the drawstring channel, beginning and ending at the opened seam.

11 Place the cover over the chair cushion. Pull the cording ends to draw up the extra fabric. Knot the cord and trim the excess cord, leaving 6" tails. Tuck the cord tails under the band.

Bartack the ends of one band joining seam, then open one side of this seam to insert the drawstring cording.

Tired of the original fabric? Turn the cover inside out, and it's dots all the way!

Ironing Day Fun

Whether it's up and in use or just hanging around, an ironing board covered in a cheerful fabric will make a fashion statement in your laundry room.

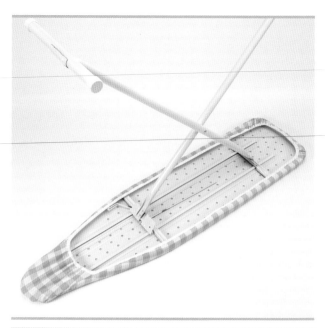

The cover extends over the board edges to the underside; a small "nose panel" secures the cover over the board's tapered end.

Materials

1 yd. of 60-wide or 1¾ yd. of 54"-wide medium-weight cotton fabric

Extra-wide double fold bias tape

Elastic cording

Instructions

1 Machine wash and machine dry your fabric before cutting it to ensure a washable cover.

2 This cover consists of two panels: a primary panel that covers the board's entire upper surface and side edges; and a "nose" panel that secures the primary panel over the board's tapered end. See the photos above for underside views of the board and this nose panel.

Trace the tapered end of the board to create the nose panel.

3 To create these panels, place your fabric, wrong-side up, on the floor. Place your ironing board, right-side down, on top of it. Trace approximately 6″ to 8″ of just the tapered end of the board; this tracing will become the nose panel.

4 Move the board at least 3″ away from this first tracing, and trace the full outline of the board; this tracing will become the primary panel.

5 To enlarge and cut the nose panel, draw a connecting line between the ends of its traced outline. Add ½″ beyond the curved edge only and cut out the enlarged panel.

6 To enlarge and cut the primary panel, first measure the depth of your board; add ½″ to this measurement. The resulting figure is the amount by which you will increase the primary panel's original traced shape. For example, if your board's depth is 1½″, you will increase the overall size of the primary panel by adding 2″ to each edge of it traced shape (1½″ + ½″ = 2″). Cut out the enlarged primary panel.

7 Stitch a double row of basting around the tapered end of the primary panel. Pull the bobbin threads to slightly gather this edge to fit the nose panel's curved edge. Pin the nose panel to the primary panel, adjusting the primary panel's gathers evenly. Stitch the panels; trim and clean finish the seam.

8 Beginning and ending in the center of the primary panel's flat edge, stitch the bias binding around the primary panel and nose panel raw edges to encase them. As you begin and end applying the bias, turn under ½″ on the bias ends and overlap them slightly.

9 Use a bodkin or safety pin to thread elastic cording through the bias channel. Turn the cover right-side out and place it over your ironing board. Pull the excess cording to create a snug fit. Double-knot the cording, trim the excess and tuck the ends inside the bias.

Appendix

You may photocopy pages 136–143 for personal use.

Furniture Dimensions Chart

(width x length in inches)

Shell Measurements

1 Inside Back .... _____ " x _____ "

2 Deck (including front/side overhang) .... _____ " x _____ "

3 Inside Arm .... _____ " x _____ "

4 Arm front .... _____ " x _____ "

5 Outside Arm .... _____ " x _____ "

6 Outside Back .... _____ " x _____ "

7 Chair Perimeter (where skirt will be attached) .... _____ "

8 Finished Skirt Length .... _____ "

9 Tuck-in Crevice Depth* .... _____ "

Box-Edge Cushion Measurements**

10 Seat Cushion Top/Bottom Panel .... _____ " x _____ "

11 Seat Cushion Box Band (cushion perimeter x depth) .... _____ " x _____ "

12 Back Cushion Top/Bottom Panel .... _____ " x _____ "

13 Back Cushion Box Band (cushion perimeter x depth) .... _____ " x _____ "

   * If the tuck-in crevice depth varies around the deck, decide on a uniform depth of between 2" to 4".

  ** If making non-box-edge cushion covers, refer to the instructions beginning on page 49 in Chapter 3 for measuring, cutting, and constructing alternative cusion covers.

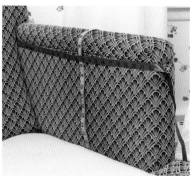

① Inside Back

② Deck

③ Inside Arm

Inside Arm Extra Width

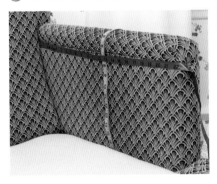

Inside Arm Extra Length

④ Arm Front

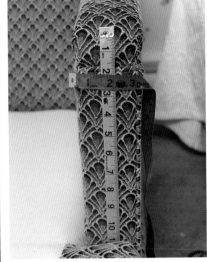

⑤ Outside Arm

⑥ Outside Back

⑦ Chair Perimeter

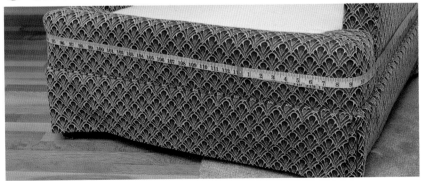

⑧ Finished Skirt Length

⑨ Tuck-In Crevice Depth

Shell and Cushion Panel Cutting Chart

(width x length in inches)

Shell Panels

1 Inside Back (cut 1)   _____" + 2" x _____" + 2" + No. 9

2 Deck, including front/side overhang (cut 1)   ____" + 3"+ (No. 9 x 2) x ____" + 3"+ No. 9

3 Inside Arm (cut 2)   _____" + 2" x _____" + 2" + No. 9

4 Arm Front (cut 2)*   _____" + 2" x _____" + 2" + No. 9

5 Outside Arm (cut 2)   _____" + 2" x _____" + 2"

6 Outside Back (cut 1)**   _____" + 2" x _____" + 2"

Box-Edge Cushion Panels***

10 Seat Cushion Top and Bottom Panel (cut 2)   _____" + 1" x _____" + 1"

11 Seat Cushion Box Band (piecing as necessary)****   _____" + 4" x _____" + 2"

12 Back Cushion Top and Bottom Panel (cut 2)   _____" + 1" x _____" + 1"

13 Back Cushion Box Band (piecing as necessary)****   _____" + 4" x _____" + 2"

Skirt Panels

Skirt panel cutting dimensions depend on the desired skirt style and allowances calculated for pleats/ gathers, seams and hems. See Skirt Panel Cutting Dimensions on the page 72 to determine the cut dimensions of panels to accommodate several common skirt styles.

---

  * These cutting dimensions include the tunck-in allowance which is required to accommodate the tutorial chair's T-shaped deck/seat cushion. For other chair/furniture styles, you will trim off some of the length of this panel during construction.

 ** If making a center back closure (in lieu of the standard back edge zipper closure), see Make Different Closures beginning on page 79 in Chapter 5 before cutting this panel.

 *** To determine the panel cutting dimensions of non-box-edge cushions, see the instructions beginning on page 49 in Chapter 3.

**** These are the overall dimensions of the box band panel for purposes of yardage calculation. For specific cutting dimensions, see Construct a Box-Edge Cushion Cover on page 45 in Chapter 3.

Skirt Panel Cutting Dimensions

Skirt Panel Cut Length
(the same for all skirt styles)

You have already determined your skirt's finished length and noted this figure as the No. 8 measurement in the Furniture Dimensions Chart on page 136. Use this figure in the following formula to determine the cut length (depth) of all of your slipcover's skirt panels; this measurement will be the same regardless of your skirt style.

panel cut length (depth) = No. 8 measurement (skirt finished length) + 4½"

For example, if you have determined that your skirt will have a finished length of 9", the cut length of the skirt panels will be 13½" (9" + 4½").

For traditional flat or pleated skirts, the extra 4½" will be used to create a 2"-deep doubled hem, and the remaining ½" will be used as the seam allowance to join the skirt upper edge to the slipcover shell's lower edge.

For skirts with welted and/or flanged, banded or scalloped hems, 3½" will be used for a hem facing panel or the hem band. The remaining 1" will be used for seam allowances to join the facing and band to the skirt lower edge and to join the skirt upper edge to the slipcover shell's lower edge.

Skirt Total Width

Start with the chair's perimeter measurement at the point where the slipcover skirt will be attached—this is the No. 7 measurement you have noted in the Furniture Dimensions Chart on page 136. To this measurement you will add pleat/gathering allowances plus seam allowances. Use inches in all calculations. *Note:* The following formulas assume a standard zipper closure.

- **For a flat skirt:** Add 8" to the No. 7 measurement. These extra inches are more than enough to join skirt panels at their short edges and stitch the remaining edges in a seam to accommodate a zipper closure.
- **For a gathered skirt:** Multiply the No. 7 measurement by 2 to 2½, depending on the desired fullness of the skirt. Add 8" to the resulting figure for joining seams and a zipper closure seam.
- **For a skirt with four box/knife-edge pleated corners** (like the tutorial chair's slipcover skirt, add 64" (16" per pleat) to the No. 7 measurement plus 8" for joining seams and a zipper closure.

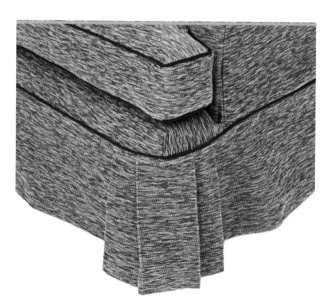

- **For a skirt with four inverted corner pleats,** add 48" (12" per pleat) to the No. 7 measurement, plus 8" for joining seams and a zipper closure.

- **For a fully pleated skirt,** first decide on the pleat style (inverted, box or knife-edge) and then determine the desired pleat depth.

  - Experiment by folding scrap fabric into pleats until you're satisfied with the pleat dimensions, then measure the desired pleat depth. (*Example:* A 6"-wide box pleat requires a 12" pleat allowance; a 3"-deep inverted pleat also requires a 12" pleat allowance; a 3"-deep knife pleat requires a 6" pleat allowance.)

  - Decide how many pleats to make (at least 8 pleats, increased by increments of 4 (that is, 8, 12, 16, 20, and so on)

  - Multiply the desired number of pleats by the determined allowance for a single pleat, and then add 8" extra for joining seams and the zipper closure. Add the resulting figure to the No. 7 measurement.

54" Layout Graph

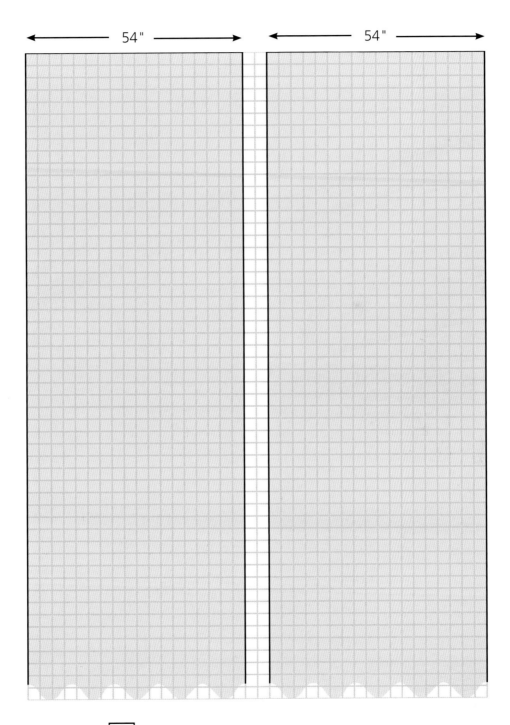

☐ = 3"

60" Layout Graph

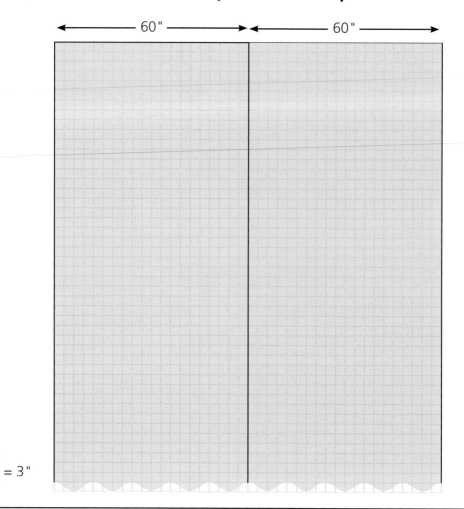

← 60" → ← 60" →

☐ = 3"

Bias Strip Yields From 1 Yard of 54"-wide Fabric

Cording Size (Approximate diameter)	Bias Width	Yield
$^6/_{32}$"	1½"	About 40 yd.
$^{12}/_{32}$"	1¾"	About 30 yd.
$^{18}/_{32}$"	2"	About 20 yd.

Fabric and Notions Shopping List:

❏ fabric for slipcover: _____ yd.

❏ fabric for welting (if different): _____ yd.

❏ muslin for inner cushion covers: _____ yd.

❏ high density upholstery foam:

  width:_____; length:_____; depth: _____

❏ quilt batting (high-loft or regular)

❏ cording size and yardage: _____ yd.

❏ zipper chain yardage: _____yd.

❏ zipper pulls/stops: _____

❏ thread

❏ machine needles, size: _____

❏ T-pins; ball head pins

❏ ⅞"-wide fusible seam/hem tape

❏ 120" tape measure

❏ water-soluble fabric marker; tailor's chalk

❏ Other Supplies:

Contributors

The following companies graciously supplied fabric and notions used in many of the projects featured in this book. To find retail and online sources for these products and to inquire about others offered by these companies, please visit the company Web sites.

Calico Corners
203 Gale Lane
Kennett Square, PA 19348
(800) 213-6366
www.calicocorners.com

Provided fabrics used in these projects (page numbers reflect primary photos): faux suede floor pillow covers, page 52; patchwork chair slipcover, pages 71 and 72; floral loveseat slipcover, pages 87 and 88; tie-on chair cover with scallop hem, pages 103-106; headboard-footboard slipcovers, page 124; library table cover, page 121.

Prym Consumer USA, Inc.
www.dritz.com

Supplied snaps and setting pliers used to create the snap closure shown on pages 79 and 80; also supplied the eyelets and setting pliers used to create the laced closure shown on page 81.

Waverly
www.waverly.com

Provided fabrics used in these projects (page numbers reflect primary photos); red twill chair cover (tutorial project), pages 8 and 9; jacquard daybed cushions, pages 40, 41 and 53; porch chair covers, page 107; porch table cover, page 110; grill cover-up, page 113; and ironing board cover, page 134.

Wrights
www.wrights.com

Supplied zipper chain, zipper pulls and stops, and cotton cording for welting, all used in numerous projects; supplied the piping used in the porch chair covers, page 107, porch table cover, page 110, grill cover-up, page 113, and dish chair reversible cover, page 131; also supplied extra-wide double fold bias tape used in the dish chair reversible cover, page 131, and in the ironing board cover, page 134.

Other Resources

Clotilde, LLC
PO Box 7500
Big Sandy, TX 75755-7500
800-772-2891
www.clotilde.com

Connecting Threads
PO Box 870760
Vancouver, WA 98687-7760
800-574-6454
www.ConnectingThreads.com

Home Sew
PO Box 4099
Bethlehem, PA 18018-0099
800-344-4739
www.homesew.com

Nancy's Notions
333 Beichl Ave
PO Box 683
Beaver Dam, WI 53916-0683
800-833-0690
www.nancysnotions.com

Krause Publications
700 E. State St.
Iola, WI 54990
800-258-0929
www.krausebooks.com

More Classic and Contemporary Customizing Tips

Christopher Nejman's Pillows
Designer Sewing Techniques
by Christopher Nejman

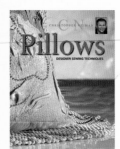

Follow charismatic instructor Christopher Nejman as he teaches you to use your punch machine to create 15 stunning designer pillows, using various threads, fabrics, and decorative stitches.

Softcover • 8¼ x 10⅞
128 pages • 225 color photos
Item# Z0304 • $22.99

No Sew, Low Sew Decorative Storage
50 Stylish Projects to Stash Your Stuff
by Carol Zentgraf & Elizabeth Dubicki

This collection of 50 inexpensive and easy-to-make storage solutions for the home can be completed with a hot glue gun, basic hand stitches, and other fast and easy techniques.

Softcover • 8¼ x 10⅞
144 pages
100+ color photos, 50 illus.
Item# DECST • $24.99

Machine Embroidery Room by Room
30+ Home Décor Projects
by Carol Zentgraf

Conduct a small-scale home makeover with themes and three design groupings for eight unique rooms, explained in 32 projects. Plus, 50 embroidery designs on a CD-ROM and a bonus monogram alphabet in two sizes.

Softcover • 8¼ x 10⅞
128 pages
200+ color photos and illus.
Item# MEHD • $29.99

101 Ways to Use Your First Sewing Machine
by Elizabeth Dubicki

Features more than 350 color photos and illustrations to lead beginning sewers through fun and practical home décor projects and stylish alterations, plus a lay-flat format provides for hands-free learning.

Hardcover w/encase spiral
8 x 8 • 192 pages
250+ color photos
Item# YFSM • $22.99

The Well-Dressed Window
Measure, Sew, Hang
by Carol Zentgraf

Save time and money while creating beautiful projects for any style of window! More than 30 exciting projects including valances, swags, shades and window treatments are covered in this new guide.

Softcover • 7 x 10
160 pages
300+ color photos and illus.
Item# SWD • $22.99

kp **krause publications**
An imprint of F+W Publications, Inc.

P.O. Box 5009, Iola, WI 54945-5009
www.krausebooks.com

● Order directly from the publisher by calling **800-258-0929** M-F 8 am - 5 pm

● Online at www.krausebooks.com, or from booksellers and craft and fabric shops nationwide.

● Please reference offer CRB7 with all direct-to-publisher orders.